Date Due

ers
nd
eed

FOREWORD

Gophers and Tumbleweed is being published posthumously in response to the requests of many readers who have enjoyed it in manuscript form.

These tales about life in southern Saskatchewan from 1915 to 1933 are autobiographical. But when he wrote the manuscript before his death in 1983, my brother Warren decided to lightly fictionalize the places and characters—perhaps because he thought no one today would believe the bizarre details of a prairie childhood during the early 1900s. However, although the names, places and some details have been changed, these stories are true—I can testify to that. The Benton family, including Bobby (Warren), Jamie (myself) and Norman (our older brother, Gerald) did indeed live in the small hamlet of Quagmire (Willows), and later moved eight miles west along the CPR line to Burdock (Assiniboia) to attend high school.

Today little has survived in Quagmire/Willows—just a deserted grain elevator and the remains of the W.G. Lowes general store. The Lowes boys, like the Bentons, have long since scattered—blown by the clouds of Depression and rumours of war. Gerald embarked on a career with the Hudson's Bay Mining and Smelting Company in Flin Flon, Manitoba; Warren went on to wartime service and a writing and journalism career. And I, perhaps in an attempt to recapture those rambling days in the coulees, eventually became involved in originating and developing Canada's Bruce Trail on the Niagara Escarpment.

The gopher has always been a common sight on the prairies,

seeming to prosper even during times of attempted extinction. The hardy tumbleweed, when the hazards of drought, cold and wind become too much to endure, breaks away from the earth and rides the winds to safer havens, spreading its seeds on the way. This book is a tribute to the indomitable spirit and resourcefulness of that generation of Canadians who grew up on the Saskatchewan grasslands during the period between the two great wars.

Like the gopher and tumbleweed, we were, above all, survivors.

Ray Lowes, O.M.C., LL.D. (Hon.)
Honorary President, Bruce Trail Association
Hamilton, Ontario, 1986

Gophers
and
Tumbleweed

TALES OF A SASKATCHEWAN BOYHOOD

Warren Lowes

Abraham Tanaka Associates

Canadian Cataloguing in Publication Data
Lowes, Warren, 1919–1983
  Gophers and tumbleweed
ISBN 0-9692375-1-0

I.   Title.
PS8573.094G66   1987   C813'.54   C87-093043-5
PR9199.3.L693G66   1987

Produced and published by
Abraham Tanaka Associates Limited, Toronto

Printed in Canada

CONTENTS

The general store.

Main street, "Quagmire,"
Saskatchewan.

Grain elevators.

The railway station.

Jamie and the coyote.

Coulee country.

Prairie winter.

*The Benton family and their
Gray Dort, ca. 1918.*

Norman, Gordon Didgey,
Jamie and Bob outside the
family home in Quagmire.

Sunday school in Quagmire.

The Benton family.

Gophers
and
Tumbleweed

1

SLEDGEHAMMER JUSTICE

*A*CCORDING to Gimpy Gaudry, Quagmire, Saskatchewan, was no place for a "city-bred prissy-pratt" to settle. And he should know, because he was the weather-beaten old weasel who had hauled the King's mail every week from Moose Jaw to the trading post at Willow Bunch. That was before the war, and before the railway came pushing through from Weyburn.

Winter blizzards were the worst hazard, when biting winds stung the flesh like a lash and turned any normal face into a piece of prairie parchment. But, with the arrival of spring, the entire scene changed. The Willow Bunch Trail wound its way down through the Dirt Hills, skirted Stink Lake and dodged newly green clumps of alders and a rash of freshly dug badger mounds until it reached Quagmire. The trail itself was often a sea of mud, but the long files of migrating waterfowl that streaked through the heavens set up a din that was music to Gimpy's ears and made the trip enjoyable.

Gimpy had survived that period, and now the railway had come to change it all. It was 1915, and the resident population of Quagmire had swollen to sixty-six, a gain of two hundred percent. One local merchant said it was a "coming town," but it still did not look like the type of place that might spawn a prime minister.

To the younger set of this village, the world was travelling in an orbit that was bounded on two sides by long shallow coulees, an expanse of alkali bottomland to the east, and the railway divisional point at Assiniboia to the west. Beyond this, the world just dropped off into some kind of limbo.

The day in question was Saturday. School was out, and the village was already filled with farm vehicles, strange dogs and people displaying a rare assortment of garb.

As usual, both general stores were crowded with farm women. Bill Benton stood behind his counter with the usual brace of pencils protruding from an overloaded vest pocket. He was a past master at keeping up a friendly banter with all and sundry who passed through his portals, while at the same time trying to keep an amateur staff fully engaged. His three barefoot sons sat on apple boxes in a side room, unpacking and counting eggs that were being taken in trade for items from the store's shelves.

"I wisht ol' Pomroy would take his stinkin' eggs somewheres else," mumbled little Jamie as he pulled his fingers dripping with the yellow slime of a broken yolk and plunged them back into the pail of oats. He was the youngest of the lads and couldn't understand why ol' Pomroy just refused to buy oyster shells to feed his hens and thus put some calcium content in their gizzards to make a stronger shell. He'd sooner squawk about the kid breaking his eggs and giving him a poor count.

Old lady Fenster was another case. She was the one who always brought her butter to market wrapped in a fancy white napkin. Once the second Benton boy, Bobby, had found a squashed bed bug in the folds of this beautiful napkin and almost caused a scene by announcing the fact loudly and in public.

"Be polite, and keep your smart remarks to yourself," warned father Bill. "We don't want her to take her business to the other store. The bugs are a bonus, so button up your lip and keep counting." In the meantime, in another corner, mother Benton busied herself at measuring off lengths of elastic from a cardboard slab while talking amiably with Mrs. Groscurth.

Some days, when business was not quite so brisk, the Benton boys preferred to escape all of this commercial wrangle by sneaking away to the blacksmith shop to watch the horses being shod, or to the livery barn to listen to the haltered teams munching their measured portions of oats. The smell of fresh manure, mice nests and sweaty harness leather seemed to complement the sound of chirping sparrows in the loft, and the ribald language of men loafing about the outer doors.

There was always a choice tidbit that could be picked up and carried back to the barn at the country school for re-telling.

But this Saturday there was a special excitement in the air. The entire focus of interest was centred on an event about to take place at Larry's Fattening Pen.

Of course, the sign hanging over the unpainted frame building read, "Muldoon's Better Foods," but women were seldom seen there and juveniles were usually told to keep away. This Saturday, however, late in the afternoon, the Benton lads were relieved of their egg-packing duties, the blinds on the windows were drawn, the doors locked and everybody went trekking off to Larry's Fattening Pen to attend "the trial."

Little clumps of people moved along the dirt walk, some trying to catch up on overheard bits of gossip and others preoccupied with the responsibilities of parenthood. There was the usual number of un-washed bare feet and, from the odd rear pocket, a slingshot or something similar might protrude—items that might better have been left at home.

"We may be going to the fattening pen," admonished Mrs. Benton, "but that's no excuse to forget your manners."

Mrs. Penfold, up ahead, pushed her little brood along without much attention to this observation and added her own. "They sure picked a fine day for these shenanigans, with George away from the stable at calving time."

The door was starting to jam up now, and the first arrivals were able to get a look at the transformation that had taken place inside. All the tables had been cleared from the floor except some small ones. They were pushed to the front, placed near the swinging doors to the kitchen. A sort of podium stood in the centre. The old showcase, which displayed its usual assortment of Sen-Sens, Zig-Zag cigarette papers, Old Chum plug tobacco and bags of Duke's Mixture, was pushed under the stairs out of the way. And the picture of the fancy floozie with the floppy hat and black garters, which usually hung above the till, had been moved off the wall altogether.

Fly-coils hung from the corrugated metal ceiling, but some new naphtha lamps had been hung, with flimsy mantels hissing out an uncertain illumination. The entire central floorspace was covered with seats—twelve-inch planks borrowed from the Superior Lumber Yard—sitting across old chairs and packing boxes. A few spitoons were scattered about the back for anyone who might be tempted to savour a pinch of "snoose."

Seating arrangements in the "court room" were "first come, first served." Kids were hustled up to the front rows where the packing boxes were lower and the planks closer to the floor. Bobby Benton noticed that in some cases planks rested on pails of Domolco Molasses, and he discussed with his brother whether or not they came from the Benton stockroom or from the opposition Gillespie store. Portly ladies like Mrs. Quintie and Maude Abernethy sought out the seats with chairs at the back; when it came to settling of parts, they afforded most support. Younger shifty types, who hung around the pool hall, preferred to stand at the back, where they could escape at the first whiff of unwashed socks, when and if the room got too hot.

After what seemed like an hour of shifting, clearing of throats, slamming of doors and loud snatches of interrupted conversation coming from the street, a strange man with dark bushy eyebrows and a noble countenance rose to his feet.

A small bell jingled, and he announced in slow sepulchral tones, *"THE COURT IS NOW IN SESSION!"*

A sense of deep solemnity seemed to settle over the crowd. The tall stranger took a sip of water from the glass before him and continued. "As Minister of the Crown, it is my duty this day to conduct hearings in the case of Rex vs. Cedric Fenimore Pool of this district, who is accused of having, on the seventh day of May, 1915, discovered, sequestered and removed from the premises of the Quagmire Clay Pit Ltd., one gold nugget of great monetary value. It is further charged that the said Mr. Pool did hide the said nugget in the basement of his domicile and subsequently made no effort to divulge the presence of this ill-gotten wealth until confronted by a committee of citizens at his home on the 14th day of June, 1915."

As the seriousness of the charges became evident to everyone, a dead hush settled over the room. The swinging doors of the kitchen opened wide and two men emerged dressed in the same kind of black robes as might be worn by the choir of the Presbyterian Church in Assiniboia. They were followed immediately by Cedric Pool, who was dressed fancier than anyone at Quagmire had ever seen him. He wore a pair of new Sunday pants from the catalogue, a blue striped shirt with detached white collar, and a silk maroon tie with light-blue forget-me-nots woven into the pattern. The deep tan on his face helped to conceal any emotions he might have felt. He was surely a different-looking fellow than the guy at the pit whom the men called "Cess" instead of Cedric.

Everybody recognized the young man in the black gown as Elmer Lloyd, the new teacher at Primrose school. Because he sat next to Mr. Pool, it was safe to say that he would be counsel for the defence.

In the front seats, sympathy for the underdog ran high from the very start. Gordon Didgey, who was eight, had explained to his friends how Cedric Pool had often allowed him to ride on his clay wagon and sometimes even to drive the big team of bays almost all the way from the pit to the unloading ramps at the railway siding—nearly three miles. The clay was blasted out in big chunks from an open pit, hauled across a long marshy grade and dumped onto flatcars at the C.P.R. siding. As many as twenty wagons would be working when they shipped the product, and the Quagmire business fraternity thought that someday it might become a major industry. Many of the village crowd didn't know exactly what became of the white solid lumps once they left Quagmire, but rumour had it they were made into crocks and pottery somewhere in Alberta.

"Now, will you take the stand, Mr. Booth, and tell the court what you saw at the clay pit on the seventh of May, 1915," the man in the other choir gown was saying. He was evidently conducting the prosecution.

And, in the witness box, poor old Cedric Pool was looking pretty green. He never did like Chester Booth, considering him just a shifty smart alec—especially since the time he had sold him a cow with four nozzles on her udder but with five holes for the milk to escape. It seemed that four streams went into the pail, and one went up his sleeve. And ol' Cedric had never forgiven him.

"Well, it was this way, your Honour. Us fellas usually take the wagons where we kin git a quick load and git away fast. I was shovelin' beside Cess there by the denimite shack and he was heavin' clay like he was a growed badger. When I lifted my eyes to look around, I catch a glint of something in the pile that sure ain't no chocolate bar wrapper."

At this juncture, the judge intervened. "In future evidence," he said, "witnesses will please refer to the accused, not as 'Cess', but as Mr. Pool or 'Cedric'."

"No offence meant, your Honour," enjoined the informant and continued. "Next time I look up, I see Mr. Pool's coat thrown over the spot, kinda lazy-way like. And in less time than it takes to pull the tail off a gopher, Cedric has picked up his jacket and he's headin' for his democrat over in the hitchin' yard. When he came back, he said he was lookin' fer his plug of MacDonald's chewin', but I noticed that he had shoved his coat an' all under the seat, way back like. Well, what would youze think of that?"

This was indeed incriminating evidence, but the worst was yet to come. People were starting to shuffle in their seats. A black mongrel dog came slinking along the rows of seats looking for his master, sniffing at everybody's legs until he had to be ushered out the closest exit.

The prosecution lawyer continued to press his case. This time he had Albert Jepsen in the witness stand. Jepsen had been with the party of citizens who searched the basement of Cedric Pool's home on June 14th when the accused was apprehended.

"We had a hunch that he would hide the mother load in the cellar," he commenced. "Mr. Pool is a natural pocket-gopher type; he collects trinkets like they was something filched from Mars. He didn't want us to see in his underground diggin's, but he kind of relented when we said we wanted to see how he was able to keep spuds down there all winter without sproutin'...guess you could say we used psychology on 'im. Well, when we got into the cellar, you can bet that we wouldn't leave 'til we had given 'er a first class checkin' out. It was Wes Tilley who spotted 'er first...right up on the top shelf beside his wife's citron preserves...just a gleamin'. We fetched 'er out, and there she is now, right over there by Jerry Culligan's anvil—Exhibit Number One!"

All eyes turned to the blacksmith's anvil, which had been positioned conspicuously in front of the podium. When the black velvet cover was removed, it revealed a gleaming hunk of treasure, fully three inches in diameter, and polished like the Crown jewels.

By this time the spirits of the beleaguered Cedric Pool were about as flat as a punctured bicycle tire. Everybody knew that criminals, like bank bandits and swindlers, got sent to prison, but here was Mr. Pool, one of the oldest customers at the Benton store, being arraigned as a common robber, and a crafty one at that. During hard times he had run up grocery bills just the same as everyone else and had paid them when the crop came off. He had taken a homestead down in the alkali flats where the only thing that would grow in the bad years was stones and sow thistle. That was why he had to haul clay as a sideline. But he was thought to be honest. In winter he loaned his team and scraper to the rink committee when they made the outdoor rink for the kids, and his wife always donated to the Willing Workers' Bake Sale.

The case was going badly and the prospects didn't seem too good, either, when the defence was called to state its case. Elmer Lloyd was a good school teacher, but he was no lawyer. Who was he to pit his wits against this distinguished stranger from who knows where?

But Elmer was now on his feet and his voice was full and confident. He lost no time in coming to the point.

"Your Honour, if it please the court," he said, "I would like to defend the honour of a citizen who has, for eight years, been a credit to this community. He is a member of the Quagmire Growers Association, a good family man, and a veteran of the Boer War. My client may have his shortcomings, like any of us, but I do not think that he is a thief!''

That was more like it. Elmer might not be able to use a lot of that high-fallutin' legal jargon, but he was saying things that went deep. Jackie Klotz, sitting next to the Benton boys and Gordon Didgey, was sitting upright and the Rodenbaugh kid was teetering on the edge of the plank.

"You have brought this man to the bar of justice, and you have charged him with a heinous crime.''

"What's 'heinous'?'' Jackie Klotz asked Gordon Didgey.

"Something awful, I think, but shut up and listen,'' came back the testy reply.

Three rows back, Maude Abernethy shifted her weight and the seat creaked.

"But where, in all of the evidence that has been presented in this courtroom,'' Mr. Lloyd continued, ''have we one shred of evidence to prove that Cedric Pool is guilty of wrongdoing? We have before us, displayed in all of its grandeur, a nugget of generous proportions—no one will gainsay that—but, you have charged my client (and your friend) of stealing gold . . . pure unadulterated *GOLD*!''

A murmur went through the crowd. Mr. Lloyd had them thinking.

"With the indulgence of the court, therefore, I propose to put this matter to the test, and to do it here and now. I have taken the liberty to commandeer the strongest man in the district to act on behalf of my client, and he is in this hall today.''

With this cue, big Jerry Culligan, the Quagmire blacksmith, came out from behind a curtain at the back and strode forward. Maybe his underwear shirt was somewhat smudgy with soot from the forge, and his black cropped hair was a bit tousled; but he had on his old leather apron with the brass rivets at the corners, and the muscles on his biceps bulged out like the superman in *Physical Culture Magazine*. Jerry Culligan didn't have to take an Earl E. Leaderman course in weight lifting. He could bite the lead out of a .303 bullet and spit it across the room. He was carrying a twenty-pound sledgehammer with him, and he headed straight for the anvil in front of the podium.

Then, before the court could consider whether or not to grant permission, and before any smart lawyer could object, Culligan hoisted his big iron mallet into the air and came down on the nugget with such a blow that it rattled all the windows in the kitchen.

Chunks and pieces flew in every direction as the nugget shattered into bits and pieces of every conceivable shape. Some fragments from the exterior, it could be easily seen, bore a veneer of shimmering gold paint, but the mass on the inside was nothing more than first-quality Quagmire pottery clay.

There was a moment of silence, then pandemonium broke loose— cheers and clapping, hoots and catcalls. It was as though armistice had been declared.

As soon as he could get order, Elmer Lloyd summed up his case in one sentence. "I'm sure that Mr. Pool has taken more clay into his kitchen on the soles of his boots after a good rain and has never been charged with robbery by his wife, Luella."

The case was thrown out of court, but that is just when the fun started.

Folks rushed over to shake hands with Cedric Pool and his teacher-lawyer from Primrose school. The freed man was wreathed in smiles. His wife, Luella, was at his side and a man was trying to manoeuvre them toward the light of the doorway so he might take some pictures with his Brownie camera. Ted Gilpin, from the Pool Elevator, said it was "a triumph for justice," and the kids who had occupied the front rows were assuring the Pool boy that they knew that his dad was not a crook all along.

While all of this fence-mending was going on, and the Pool family was being eagerly embraced by the community again as upright citizens, another deputation was busy clearing benches back to the walls and bringing in tables for food. Women from the Lutheran Auxiliary carried boxes of sandwiches and numerous cakes, while Larry Muldoon had a huge pot of coffee bubbling on the kitchen range. The way everything fell into place, one would think that the whole affair had been orchestrated from some mysterious headquarters, but it was merely custom born of tradition.

And the wellsprings of community goodwill bubbled in unison with the coffee. The War was in its second year, and some young men were already in the service overseas. Three ladies from the local choir started the sing-song and there were rousing choruses from *Britannia Rule the Waves* and *We'll Never Let the Old Flag Fall*, sung with a patriotic fervour that fairly lifted the shingles on the fattening pen roof.

Then old Charlie Rainville opened up his fiddle case, sawed out a few bars of *The Fisherman's Hornpipe*, and Rafe Pinder took to the step-dancing. Things just went from one thing to another until a square dance was in full swing and nothing could be heard in the street but the shuffle of feet and the recurring swells of music as violin, banjo and drum moved easily from two-steps to quadrilles.

The trial of Cedric Pool was over and all sense of recrimination wiped out—if, indeed, it had existed in the first place. To some of the citizenry, something of a mystery about the whole thing lingered.

But, as time went on, pieces gradually started to fit together. There was no write-up and no photograph of Mr. Pool in the *Assiniboia Times*, as some had expected. Lively discussions were sometimes abruptly ended when juvenile ears chanced to intrude. But, Bill Benton, the guardian of village decorum, put it all into context when he remarked one day to a travelling salesman in the general store, "Manufacturing crime, to some galoots, is more fun than the real thing."

Could it be that the whole affair was a hoax? At the school teachers' convention that fall in Burdock, it was noted that one of the out-of-town delegates was that tall dark man with the bushy eyebrows and the noble look on his face.

Yes, the windswept prairie sometimes blew up social twisters of its own.

2

TAMPERING WITH THE HOLY GRAIL

*T*HE trial at Quagmire that spring had stirred up talk about just how far the teachers should become involved with the "less responsible elements of the community." But school was now out, controls were off, and adult supervision had almost ceased. The tribal underlings of Quagmire had become a fraternity of wandering free spirits.

One night Norman was asked to go to the Ramshaw farm the following day. He would be riding a big flat-backed Percheron mare while Ramshaw plodded down the long rows of potatoes behind a rusty old cultivator. There would be some spending money in prospect, of course, but Norman was more interested in the array of pies and desserts at Martha Ramshaw's table.

Bob and little Jamie, the two younger brothers, were not needed for this job and felt a small twinge of rejection.

"Ramshaw's horses stink of sweat," Jamie said. "He only asks us when he has some yucky job like feedin' dusty wheat into some ol' fanning mill like we did this spring."

But now these labour market rejects had their own plans for the day as they packed sandwiches, fig Newtons, a few hanks of string, a rusty knife and other assorted oddments into a battered pack-sack.

By nine o'clock the morning air was warm and dry, and the sky was big and blue except for the high drifting puffs of cloud that moved slowly eastward to the prairie's edge. Crows were calling back in the coulee. There were still a few pot-holes of alkali water filling the lower spots of the creek bed, a reminder of the spring run-off long since gone. And even if the swimming was somewhat restricted, there would always be something to investigate among the reeds and tall grasses—water beetles, mating frogs, nesting ducks, muskrat huts, or possibly one of those brown spindly-legged water birds that sometimes flew out of the marsh, leaving a long streak of excrement in the air. Lignite Joe, who lived near the old coal-mine shaft, called them "shite pokes."

Bobby and Jamie left the Benton house with a big clumsy mutt of a dog on their heels. Toby, a suspect collie of uncertain pedigree, had little respect for protocol and was crowding everybody into the picket fence, lashing pant-legs with his free-swinging tail. A moment later, he was walking all over Mrs. Keeler's nasturtiums and brushing against the trellised sweet peas outside the house where Gordon Didgey lived. Gordon's mother always slept late, so they knew from previous experience that they would have to peer through the kitchen window and possibly catch him at breakfast, rather than rap at the door.

But this time Gordon had been waiting in anticipation for a half-hour or more, impulsively stuffing his face with everything in sight. The day was fresh and inviting. It could be a long time before supper.

"Got any gum with you?" were the first words of greeting as Gordon emerged into the alley and the screen door banged shut behind him.

"Nope! But if some skunk don't find them first, there should be plenty of chocolate bars when we get back to the cache," Bobby confirmed.

With this assurance, the trio crossed the street followed by Toby and entered the alley behind the Gillespie store where they were to meet Tuffy Parsons and his cousin, who was said to be visiting from faraway Crane Valley.

Right on schedule, there was Tuffy—but they didn't expect that his cousin was going to be a *girl*.

"Bernice can do cartwheels," Tuffy announced by way of an introduction. "At Crane Valley, she is the championship."

The little tow-headed girl smiled. "My dad runs the livery barn, and we also raise pigs," she added as further words of commendation. She scuffed the loose dirt with her bare foot and concluded with a note of pride, "My name is Bernice Raymer."

She then announced that she could also do handsprings. Furthermore, she proceeded to demonstrate these talents right there in the alley. As they all stood with mouths agape, Toby leaped in wide circles and managed to get his head in the way as Bernice tried to finish her routine in the splits.

No further testimonial was needed. Bernice was accepted into the brotherhood. But, before they moved off, Gordon Didgey decided to check out what all they had brought in their packs. Some sandwiches, a lot of gingersnaps and a hunting knife—just what they needed. Toby sniffed again at the girl's heels and the little troop moved off over the prairie, back to the coulee and toward the railway trestle.

There was a warmer breeze blowing now, causing skittish shimmers to run along the tops of the long grass. As they followed a little-used wagon track, the children were only partially aware of the continuous symphony of sounds and smells that engulfed them. They had experienced it all before and in a sense had become part of it. A long-legged meadowlark, with bright yellow breast-plate fully expanded, practised arpeggios with endless enthusiasm. Here and there a clump of yarrow carried a blob of goo left by a spittle bug. Then there came a moment of stillness, to be abruptly punctuated by the high-pitched chirp of a gopher who had just made it to the safety of its burrow with a breathless Toby in hot pursuit.

Up ahead, a long ravine led to the wider, flattened-out coulee below. The little band moved along until the trail itself disappeared into clumps of chokecherry and Saskatoon bushes that grew like pubic adornment along the folds of the hills. It was here that both they and the Indian kids before them had come to pick berries in August. Oldtimers said these hills and draws had once been good places to gather buffalo chips, but that day had passed.

Over on a grassy knoll, Gordon Didgey was crouched down on his haunches, poking vigorously into an ant-hill with a stick.

"Hey! You guys!" he shouted. "Don't you remember? This is the place where we left the dead rabbit ta git processed."

They all gathered around while he prodded a little deeper, and the wafts of mouldy putrefaction carried upward upon the breeze. Toby had his nose poked into the scene of disorder and had gone a bit spooky from the sensation of ants crawling into his mouth and over the end of his muzzle. He was still too much of a pup to have learned the meaning of discretion.

"This is jist what we wanted," Gordon announced with enthusiasm. "A perfect skeleton. See how the ants have eaten all the meat off the bones. Not even any guts or eyeballs left."

"They even ate the poop," added little Jamie.

It was Gordon who had initiated the experiment about a month previously, and he was elated with the results. Bernice, however, did not seem to have the stomach for such research, so had wandered off into the bushes. She was sitting on a stump, nursing Tuffy's lunch pail, but the boys were not to be distracted by her. Gordon Didgey and Bobby Benton had found a flat board along the fence line and were laying out the skeleton very carefully.

"Next comes the bleaching process," Gordon explained. "We'll leave it in the sun now and come and get it later—maybe tomorrow. Also, we can bring a sheet of glass and put it crossways through the ant hill, like they show in *The Chums Annual*. Then we can come and watch how the ants run their town."

It was an intriguing prospect, but Tuffy had wandered away, and so had Toby. They were over conversing with Bernice—at least Tuffy was—while the brindle pup lolled out full length in the grass and occasionally nuzzled his parts.

Sitting in the shade, with nothing particular to occupy their attention while the mid-morning breezes blew languid and warm, it was almost preordained that the lunch pails would come out. It wasn't that there was any need for food; they had not been away for more than half an hour. But there was always the gnawing compulsion to start nibbling when edibles were in reach. This brought Gordon and Bobby around, and they were eating their share of gingersnaps and fig Newtons when Toby wandered out of the berry bush with sprigs of straw clinging to the long shaggy hair on his chest. He was being escorted along by the excited and scornful chatter of a kingbird who swooped and dived at his head persistently. Toby had, no doubt, intruded into the private nesting preserve of his assailant.

The entire party moved quickly to the new point of interest and discovered where a broken bale of wheatstraw had once been scattered about the ground near an overhang of wolf willow.

"Must be a pirate's lair or something," Jamie remarked with a tone of manufactured wonder. But Tuffy had moved on by himself to investigate the whereabouts of the kingbird's nest farther up the ravine.

He returned shortly carrying a single egg in his open hand.

"What did you go an' do that screwy thing fer?" Gordon demanded.

"I wonder how these eggs git turned into birds. Maybe we can find out," Tuffy answered with a guilty grin.

"That's stupid," snapped Gordon. "They just hatch."

31

Well, even little Jamie knew more than that. He had watched his mother clean a chicken for Sunday dinner a few times and had learned how the rooster put a germ in the centre of each egg before it came out of the hen.

"And there's a germ right in the kingbird's egg right in your hand," Bobby added in full support.

Tuffy didn't take the declaration for gospel truth. He sat down beside Bernice Raymer on the straw and carefully cracked open the shell. Sure enough, there was a small cloud of a thing attached to the yolk.

"That's going to be a baby bird," said Jamie, crowding his face in a little closer.

"I guess it ain't gonna be now," added Tuffy with a note of remorse. "But how did it git in there in the first place?"

"The kingbird's husband put it there with his dicker, stupid!" Bobby shot back.

Tuffy Parsons might have been the oldest one of the five kids, but he was more bewildered than ever by this remark. "Who ever saw a kingbird with its dicker hangin' out?" he blurted.

"But they got 'em. And the lady kingbird isn't called a queenbird, either, but she's got a kahoozie," little Jamie added as though he was throwing down a trump card.

Tuffy just stood there, bewildered and somewhat embarrassed.

"All boy animals have got dickers, and girls have kahoozies, and that goes for birds, too," Gordon repeated with an air of finality. "If you don't believe it, ask your cousin Bernice."

Well, that was the last straw. Tuffy wasn't going to be held up for ridicule before the other Quagmire crowd, so he turned to Bernice and asked his question with direct bluntness. "If you got one of those things they're talkin' about, why don't you show it to us?"

Bernice blushed slightly, giggled nervously and pulled at Toby's generous tail. Was turning cartwheels not enough? Was this all part of belonging to the brotherhood? Hesitatingly, she lifted her gingham skirt and yanked at the elastic. Everyone, including Toby, took a close look, and the discussion ended in silence. From her eye, the little gymnast wiped a tear.

"Gee, I thought there would be a stem," ventured Jamie after a moment.

Ten minutes later, when the little troop emerged from the Saskatoon grove, Toby was eagerly awaiting. His face was covered with mud and his tongue tumbled out the side of his mouth, dripping saliva all over his tawny chest. He had been experiencing the utter futility of trying to dig a gopher out of its hole. Not that he hadn't excavated enough earth with his nose and flailing paws; the evidence was there for all to see. But what he hadn't seemed to realize was that the gopher had long since departed through an adjoining tunnel.

Now the panting pup was ready to lead the expedition onward, to the floor of the coulee and down to the edge of a creek bed that had been gouged out by centuries of spring drainage. A few pools of motionless water sat in the low spots, each fringed by a light skirting of white alkali, and these held the last promise of a murky swim.

As though by tribal custom, the boys started hauling clothes over their heads even before they had reached the bank. Even Jamie, who had been warned against swimming on account of his rashes. As they tumbled into the water, tossing out garter snakes, Toby forged far ahead, sending out long streamers and demonstrating the original dog-paddle. Everybody was flailing water in some fashion. Everybody, that is, except Bernice...she just walked along the bank by herself and munched a cookie. Nobody knew whether she didn't want to get wet, was scared of the garter snakes, or didn't like to get her bare skin all covered with alkali mud.

Bernice wandered along the creek to where some red-winged blackbirds were flying in and out of a clump of bulrushes and sending up a clacking babble. A lone kildeer ran along the shore, halting abruptly from time to time to pick off a bug or a wandering spider.

"What's wrong with her, I wonder?" Bobby Benton ventured.

"Jist girls," said Gordon Didgey. "They're not like us even if she is Tuffy's cousin. I'll bet she goes and tells your mother when she gits home."

That last remark was directed at Tuffy, and he knew it. "She kin tell all she likes," he answered. "She didn't have to come in the first place if she doesn't like doin' what we do."

Somehow it seemed pointless to remain in the water when everybody was so irritated, so the four nudists pulled their shirts and pants back on. They were ready to resume the trek, this time along the face of the coulee running north from Quagmire. Bernice followed at a measured distance, pretending to play with Toby.

About a mile ahead, and just before the coulee reached the lake, two other ravines entered the drainage system, creating some rough wasteland. It was there that the "cache" had been concealed in an abandoned dugout near an unused gravel pit. Just over the brow stood a vacant tarpaper shack. Looking back, they noticed that Bernice had caught sight of the Quagmire elevators, and was now heading for home.

"Let 'er go," said Tuffy with misgivings. "We'll go up to where the cache is and eat the rest of our lunch."

A quarter of an hour later, pieces of rusty sheet-metal were being lifted away from the mouth of a small excavation set in the side of a hummock and partially concealed by a clump of wild roses, now in full bloom. Inside, it was apparent that foraging field mice had made a mess of the box of cracker-jack, but a metal Red Ribbon Tea container, with its tight lid, still protected its prize of eight chocolate bars, some matches and a box of raisins. It was not long before the lads were stuffing themselves, in the delight that can only come from food that has a clandestine origin.

Moments later they were all sprawled out on the grass, bellies full, and with the summer sun pouring down its warmth and blessing. Tuffy, while studying the wart on the back of his hand, ventured a thought that had been running through the other tousled heads for some time. "I wonder what's in that ol' shack with the gunny-sack curtains over the other side of this hill?"

There was a long pause. "A guy used to live in that place last fall, but he went away," Bobby finally volunteered. "I heard some men talking in the blacksmith shop and they said he worked in some mine in B.C."

"How come he has a shack here and works in B.C.?" asked Gordon, not really expecting an answer.

"Well," continued Bobby, "how do I know? His name is Steve Sikora an' he's a mean fighter. I know that, anyway."

"Did you ever see one of those miner's lights they strap on their heads when they go underground into the dark?" inquired Tuffy, away on a new track altogether.

"They put acetylene stones or something into the bottom part, and you wet them, and when some gas fizzes up off the stones, you light it some way," added Gordon. "I saw some in Cape Breton when we lived in Dominion, but I didn't see one right up close."

A fervent discussion on the care and handling of miners' lamps ensued. Any onlooker could easily have got the impression that they were talking about some secret sort of spirit decanter handed down by members of an ancient Persian priestly cast—a kind of mystic Holy Grail.

"Maybe Mr. Sikora left one of those in his shack, and we could look at it," Tuffy speculated aloud.

Well, it was an appealing thought. In a short moment, Toby was leading the way down the path through patches of sage and wild gooseberry bushes, until they arrived at the old building with torn pieces of tarpaper flapping in the breeze and a rusty padlock securing the sun-parched wooden door.

The whole place carried the atmosphere of dejection. Long grass grew between the flat shale slabs in front of the door, while stands of goldenrod and sow thistle grew rank under the windows. There were gaping holes under the foundation at both ends, and an unmistakable odour of skunk.

Tuffy rattled the lock while the other three stood back watching. When nothing happened, each carried out a different avenue of inspection. Tuffy, however, remained intrigued by the lock. He noticed that the jamb of the door was badly weathered, and that the screwnails were not too tight in their sockets. Possibly a little persuasion was all that was needed. He removed the rusty hunting knife from his pack, inserted it between the jamb and the sill and began to wiggle.

The hasp with its lock still attached fell to the ground, and the door creaked open.

For a moment they all stood transfixed, looking into the gloomy interior. The smell of skunk now blended with the dank aroma of musty mouse nests and remnants of stale food. The stove-pipe through the roof led to a rusty flat-topped range backed by its complement of smoky pots and a frying pan hung from nails in the wall. There was little else in the room but a cot, a couple of apple boxes, a rickety table, some issues of *Police Gazette* scattered over the floor, and an assortment of odd dishes on a shelf. Pinned to the wall was a faded newspaper clipping featuring a boxer in shorts, posed in the crouch position. A caption under the picture read: "Wildcat Sikora Stalks His Prey."

By this time all the kids were inside the shack, eager to snoop but ready for a quick exit. There was a feeling of spookiness about the place. Tuffy and Gordon ventured farther in and were about to go back when Gordon stopped to look at an assortment of rock samples, some scraps of leather and some rusty tins together with a liberal scattering of mouse droppings on a stand near the back wall.

There it was among the debris—the Holy Grail itself, with full headgear attached.

Tuffy pushed forward, lifted it out of its setting and they all started for the door.

"Here, hold this while I fix the lock," he beckoned, handing the treasure to Gordon.

To replace the hasp was a simple matter; the screwnails slipped back into the original holes, and a few taps with a small rock set them in place.

Up to this point, little Jamie hadn't said a word, but he was first in line as they all walked Indian-file down the path toward the hummock where they had eaten lunch. "This is stealin', isn't it?" he asked.

Once back at the cache, the next consideration was whether or not to try to get the magic lamp in operation. Tuffy went for the matches in the old Red Ribbon Tea canister. Meanwhile, Gordon and Bobby busied themselves removing a part attached to the lower section of the lamp.

"There's a few lumps of some kinda junk in here," Gordon announced. "But what do we use to get it makin' gas?"

Nobody had an answer. Did you use coal oil, or turpentine? Or could it even be water?

Since they didn't know, and since they didn't have any kind of liquid available, anyway, they were eventually forced to a decision—not to decide now. The lighting-up ceremonies would have to be put over until they could get more information and the right kind of juice. They would have to come again.

"We can't take it home, because people will ask where it came from," said Gordon Didgey with concern. "So I guess we'll have to leave it in the dugout with the other stuff until we come back some time next week." That seemed the better part of reason, so they all agreed.

With the big decision made, there seemed little need to waste time in dalliance. Before ten minutes had passed, they were on the brow of the hill and moving onto the flat expanse of prairie again, with the grain elevators of Quagmire within easy sight.

Patches of foxtail brushed their legs and the broad-leafed plantain made a good cushion for bare feet. At times, the odd shaft of spear grass might pierce through the thin wall of an undergarment and irritate the skin, but that was a minor nuisance. The air was still, the silence broken only occasionally by the far-off whistle of a plover or the billowing chorus of buntings on the wing. It was almost mid-afternoon, a time when little waves of heat seemed to shimmer and dance along the horizon. The little band was picking its way toward the village, deep in thought.

By the time they had reached the community hall at the outer boundary, it became manifest to everyone that there was a need to swear each other to deep secrecy concerning all details of the very questionable adventure in which they had all been implicated. But feelings of honour and guilt seemed to be in such conflict that the subject was not even broached. In fact, it went unmentioned even when Tuffy Parsons broke off from the group, deciding to go home by the shortest route, the alley.

Up ahead, at the blacksmith shop, a group of men had gathered around the open door, and black smoke was belching from the chimney. Somebody was getting the steel rims off some dried-out wagon wheel re-set, and big Jerry Culligan's forge was pumping out the heat. The trio approached with the usual air of innocence and charm.

In one group, some farmers seemed to be absorbed in a series of conversations about the prospects of a wheat crop, and one man was heard to say that "anything that ain't two weeks into the shot-blade now is a goner."

"Why should any gol-denged politician tell me how and when to market my hogs," came the high-pitched voice of Elmo Phrimmer, who was always yammering about "interference in the marketplace."

Snatches of conversation were coming from all directions. "Did ya git a mate fer that roan mare yet?" "I figger on clearin' the stones off that whole quarter-section." "It costs more to feed turkeys in the shed, but they taste a hell of a lot better runnin' in the fields an' pickin' up grasshoppers." "They say his Mrs. left him an' went back to Nova Scotia."

All this jumble of talk was not of much interest to the boys—just dull farmer chatter they had heard many times before. Not, that is, until they picked up a fragment of conversation that came from a man sitting on an overturned nail-keg, leaning against the north wall. He was talking to another man from Readlyn, whom they did not know.

"Did ya hear Steve Sikora is back in the country? Saw him in Assiniboia Tuesday. Said he'd be down tomorrow. Looks good. Been winning some fights."

Some young ears picked up pretty briskly on that one! They listened intently to glean any further snatches of information that might be forthcoming, but the remainder of the conversation was lost in the babble of voices. They made a quiet withdrawal.

That night, in the quiet of one Benton bedroom at least, there didn't seem to be much chance of sleep. Before going to bed, both Bobby and Jamie had gone through the prescribed ritual of washing dirty feet without a semblance of goading from Louisa Benton, their mother. She liked to see the boys growing strong and healthy in the open air, and the fact that they chose to stay a full day in the coulees by themselves bespoke a degree of self-reliance that made her feel proud. They were, in her eyes, true sons of the homesteaders.

But Jamie, under the blankets, did not feel like the son of anything much braver than a field mouse. He cuddled up closer to Bobby, pulled the flannelette blankets over his head to ensure complete privacy, and whispered in a guarded wheeze, "What if that Steve Sikora guy has come back to git his lamp?"

"It was all Tuffy Parsons' fault," Bobby answered in the same stifled whisper. It was about the best thing he could think of to say.

Later, Bobby toyed with the idea of getting dressed and sneaking over to Parsons' house to confront him with the news, but was afraid of waking someone and causing an alarm. "Gordon Didgey usually has good ideas," he mused. "I wonder what he is thinking about?" No answer. The room was silent.

The big kitchen clock downstairs made its announcement at eleven, and again at midnight. Then there was the sound of footsteps when Aunt Mabel made her nightly pilgrimage to the toilet. Long silences followed, and as the moments stretched into periods of blank bewilderment, Bobby became conscious of the fact that he was alone. The soft breathing beside him was a sure sign that sleep had carried his brother off to slumberland.

At first it seemed strangely unfair that he should have to face his conscience alone. Was this possibly part of the punishment? If so, it was indeed a fantasy to be dispelled as quickly as possible, as he thought of events earlier in the day, looking for something more pleasant to contemplate. He could picture himself stretched out in the deep grass watching the white clouds drifting aimlessly. He could feel Toby licking at his hand and the warm earth soothing his back. And that was the magic wand that finally lowered the curtain of sleep.

But even if that sleep did obscure events of the day, it also distorted them. What the waking hours of the conscious mind can contemplate, the devilish hours of delirium can twist and tangle.

Bernice Raymer was a nice girl whose mother had even taught her how to make her own school dresses. Why, then, in this veil of hallucination, was she standing on the roof of a tarpaper shack with no clothes on whatsoever, and Mr. Sikora trying to haul her down? Is that why they called him "wildcat"? The screams could be heard even back at the gravel pit, but Tuffy didn't even seem to care.

Gordon Didgey was quietly sneaking up behind the pugilist, carrying a rough board with a wicked spike sticking out of it. He was just going to whack the villain over the head when something seemed to start pulling him into a hole. In his nightmare, Bobby felt the same pull. And the hole was full of slimy water. And the water was alive with green frogs and slithery garter snakes. And the sucking went on and on, but neither of them sank beyond the belly-button.

While this was all going on, Jamie came out of the shack carrying a lighted miner's lamp. Tuffy came running over the hill, grabbed it out of his hands and was about to set fire to some tarpaper flapping in the wind on the wall.

"Don't do it!" Bobby yelled. "Bernice is on the roof!"

He awoke with a jerk, and when the clouds of horror lifted, he found Jamie tugging at his shoulder and chucking his chin.

"Are you fellows all right in there?" came the voice of father Benton from the adjoining room.

Nobody answered. Nobody went back to sleep again, either. And that nobody was Bobby Benton.

The clock struck four. In an hour and a half the sun would be starting to come up and the first rays of sunlight would show. If anything was going to be done, it would have to be done soon.

At five o'clock, Bobby eased himself out of bed as quietly as possible, dressed and tiptoed downstairs in his bare feet.

Gordon Didgey, he knew, lived not far away and in the summertime slept on the screened verandah.

It didn't take much to arouse him. He, too, so it seemed, had spent a bad night.

As they headed back over the prairie that morning, the sun was pushing its first shafts of light over the eastern horizon. A rooster crowed in Parsons' chickenhouse. As they cut through Mrs. Keeler's yard, it was necessary to skirt some clothes she had left on the line overnight, but there was evidently no one up and around, so the coast was clear. They came out on the vacant lot and knew there would be nobody around the community hall. From there it was a cinch that they could make the coulee unnoticed.

With bare feet and pant legs damp from running through the grass, they arrived at the cache in exactly twenty minutes. In another ten minutes the lock had been wiggled from its moorings and the miner's lamp was back on its shelf among the rocks and other clutter. Hardly a mouse dropping was disturbed.

The trip back to Quagmire, too, was somewhat of a record. Fortunately ol' man Pinder, who usually milked his cow at an unearthly hour, was in the shed along with his lighted lantern and a pail of slop for the pig. The mission had been accomplished.

When Bobby returned to his room, Jamie was still curled up in his flannelette blanket. He stirred at the dip of the yielding bed-spring. An unintentional bunt on the rump finished his repose. His eyes opened wide.

"Where you bin all by yourself?" he muttered, propping himself up on one elbow and pulling away from Bobby's cold feet.

It was no time for loud talk, so Bobby drew the blankets over their heads and breathlessly explained the details of the early morning mission.

At the breakfast table, an hour later, Louisa Benton caught a glimpse of Bobby's lower extremities. "Don't tell me that you got into my clean sheets last night with grubby-looking feet like those," she chided.

Bobby bit his lip and just grinned. That might be dumb, he thought to himself, but not as dumb as Tuffy Parsons, who must still be unaware of the real drama concerning the fate of the Holy Grail. He just seemed to miss out on everything.

3

THE TROUBLE WITH SIN

*T*HE community hall at Quagmire
served many purposes, but the church services held there on Sunday
mornings constituted a leavening force, a counterbalance to the effer-
vescent suffusion of sin, which seemed to well up out of the prairie soil
like spring mushrooms.

Take the time when ol' Rip Hogan at the livery stable got a few
cronies together on Sunday morning and tied a string of tin cans to the
tail of Jack Pomroy's bull. Just about the time church was coming out,
they turned the bull loose and headed him for home, which was across
the coulee back of the community hall. As he passed the congregation,
with his bellowing and the unholy clatter of cans, it seemed an act that
showed little respect for the bull and even less for the church-going
people of Quagmire. Mr. Hogan should have known better, too. At
least you would expect something better from the proprietor of the
livery stable and a member of the Board of Trade.

Within the Benton household there was also a tangle of interests
and concerns. Bill Benton, as one of the local merchants, knew that
"right thinking" people paid their grocery bills. Louisa Benton had
discovered that bringing up three boys on the flat prairie wasn't as easy
as it might have been in her former Methodist surroundings in Welling-

ton County "down east." Thus, the Benton establishment became a Mecca for all travelling missionaries traversing the country. When services were made possible, full family attendance was mandatory.

The Reverend Gow came occasionally from the Mission Alliance and that meant going to the community hall as many as three times at a visit—visits that invariably came when the wide open spaces were calling, the gophers back in the coulee were running wild and Toby the dog was eager to romp and give them full attention.

The Benton boys liked the church music, but the restrictions to their summer exploits seemed almost too much to endure.

"Why do we have to listen to that Mr. Gow tellin' all about floods drownin' out people in Jerusalem or somewhere?" Norman once said. "The swimmin' at the C.P.R. dam washes all our sins away." Then Gordon Didgey would aggravate the situation by explaining that the story he liked best "is where there is a great miracle on the side of a hill and everybody loafs an' fishes."

On Sunday, Mr. Lindquist, from a nearby farm, would bring a pump-up organ to the hall in the back of a wagon-box. The men of the congregation would unload it carefully and push it up to the front, just to the right of the pulpit. The hymn singing that followed would be so fervent and glorious that any trace elements of sin around that place would certainly feel unwelcome. But that still was not enough for the younger element.

Bobby and little Jamie liked to sit behind Mrs. Engstrom from Crane Valley, particularly when they started to sing "Jesus Saves." With her particular dialect of English mixed with Norwegian, the message, to Jamie's ear, sounded more like "Yesus Shaves," leading to uncontrolled fits of snickering. Louisa had to watch the situation closely.

Then, every three or four weeks, a Miss Keatch came to stay at the Benton house for a few days. In the morning, just before she had to leave for the next charge, the kids all had to get together while she taught them songs of faraway India—the same songs she had learned in the mission fields at Calcutta. They were all in Bengalese and some passages could be committed to memory, but, as Gordon Didgey said, "The Indian kids at Willow Bunch never heard them before and they think we're nuts." Another thing they couldn't understand about Miss Keatch was the way she rode her old roan mare, Daisy. When she was leaving Quagmire, wearing her funny peaked bonnet, she rode side-saddle, but when she got past the tracks on the other side of the elevators, she switched over to cowboy style. They thought all West-erners should ride cowboy style.

But, with all of this exposure to the finer elements of life, especially imported to add moral fibre, there remained that problem of coping with the more subtle forces of evil on the home front. Just what shenanigans went on at the livery stable to corrupt and debauch? The thing that aggravated the Benton lads and their friends was that they were not allowed to go there to investigate. How did anyone expect them to root out sin and fight it to the ground unless they could find out just where it lurked?

During the previous year, the southern Saskatchewan wheatlands had delivered a bumper crop. Prospects for another bonanza were bright again, and it was on the strength of this promise that Bill Benton brought his cousin, Dalton, out from Ontario to help in the store and to survey the prospects of settling in the West. He was to eat with the family and sleep in the big empty room over the store. Benton thought it was a good idea to have somebody sleep in the building in case some wandering ne'er-do-well might try to make entry at night. What he didn't tell Dalton was that the missionaries sometimes slept there, too.

Of course, the boys expected that if he was their father's cousin, he would be an amiable sort. When he arrived, however, they weren't so sure. Dalton seemed to know only two things—how to say no with conviction, and how to argue and always win.

He had a sad, round face, small tufts of hair protruding from his ears, and his head was as bald as the prairie on Soaring Eagle Butte. When he frowned, even the top of his naked dome would wrinkle with concern, and when he argued, bits of foamy spittle collected in the corners of his mouth.

Bobby and Jamie Benton put him under the closest surveillance at once. On bright days he squinted quite a bit, possibly from the abundance of sun unimpeded by trees and tall buildings. His legs were too short for him to be much of a runner. But his short chubby hands looked pretty powerful. The first test, of course, would come on Saturday, when the store was busy and it was customary for them to snitch a few handfuls of goodies from the candy pails in the stock room. The usual procedure was to sit on the pails while unpacking eggs, slide the cover forward and fill the back pockets without losing count. Thus the hidden cache back in the coulee could be constantly replenished, and ol' Dalt would never know.

Well, ol' Dalt didn't know at first, but it didn't take long for him to guess that losses were being incurred. He started weighing the pails before and after Saturday's business and it was only a matter of time before the jig was up. "I'll tell you, Bill," he said one day. "These kids are eating you out of business, to say nothing of what is happening to their teeth."

Norman heard the remark and relayed it down the line.

"Ye'd think he owns the place," exploded Bobby at the first revelation. "Is he gonna count all the jelly-beans every night an' lock 'em in the safe? The ol' coot!"

Norman wasn't so sure they had a case. Possibly some of the sermons he heard at the community hall were starting to seep into the folds of his adolescent mind.

"Maybe he is on the side of righteousness and knows about the Ten Commandments like the Rev. Gow talks about. Maybe Uncle Dalt is pure and the evil is in us," he conjectured. "You'll have to consider that."

Well, the very next week ol' Dalt had a chance to prove whether or not he was motivated entirely by divine guidance.

Louisa Benton had supper ready and insisted that the boys carry out the usual ablutions, including neck and ears. They were all ready to sit down when Bill Benton and Dalton entered, accompanied by a strange man dressed in clerical collar and a dark grey suit. The man smiled while he looked about for a place to set his black fedora hat. The boys had never seen one of these before. They also noticed that his shoes were polished shinier than any they had ever seen at Quagmire.

"This is Dr. Toomey, all the way from St. Thomas, Ontario," Benton announced. "He is making a trip through the Western Mission Fields, and has just dropped in to say hello."

Mrs. Benton was somewhat taken aback by the sudden appearance of a visitor at mealtime, but she regained composure by moving chairs about and pushing the coal scuttle behind the stove. Then she summoned Norman, the most dependable of the three boys, and dispatched him on a quick trip to the store for two tins of red sockeye salmon, while she opened a jar of peach preserves that were usually kept for emergency situations.

All of this time, Bill Benton engaged Dr. Toomey in a probing conversation during which such terms as "Development Fund" and "Quarterly Official Board" were mentioned with some solemnity. To Bobby and Jamie, who had been schooled in the social imperative of being seen-but-not-heard, these terms were meaningless—they just noticed a fly that was trying to land on his nose. Somehow they had become familiar with such phrases as "the power of redemption" and "the wages of sin," and even "the trumpets of the Lord," by listening to the Reverend Gow. But, they reasoned, this new talk must have something to do with what made the difference between a reverend and a doctor.

"Such a delightful treat to get away out here on the Western

Plains," said the wayfaring prelate, obviously relishing the red salmon with scalloped potatoes. "We consider ourselves lucky to taste such delicacy even in old Ontario."

Bobby and Jamie had been effectively silenced by house protocol, but Norman knew exactly what both of them were thinking—(salmon is no great deal at this table on account of it comes by freight from B.C. and we get it every time visitors appear out of the blue).

The meal proceeded without a hitch. Louisa got out her special pinafore—the one Miss Keatch had brought from Ceylon. When she poured tea, Bobby noticed, the little finger on her right hand was curled tighter than a fiddlehead fern breaking through the earth in spring, and there were sugar lumps on the table in the special flowered bowl that came from Auntie Millicent in Ontario. The boys also noted that, through all of this discussion about Quarterly Official Boards and such, ol' Dalt was as silent as they. He even faked closing his eyes when Dr. Toomey said the grace.

"I hope you weren't thinking of going on tonight?" father Benton inquired, as the supper dishes were being cleaned away. "We don't have palatial quarters to offer here, but there is an extra bed in the spare room where Dalton sleeps, if you care to stay with him."

With this suggestion, Dalton perked up, and a sort of pink flush billowed up out of his shirt collar, ran past his ears and right across his bald head. He made a kind of snicky noise, like Toby might make if a husk of beardy wheat stuck in his nose. He looked very uncomfortable.

"Well, you've put my horse away on me. I suppose there is a need to be frugal when we are out doing the Lord's work," said Dr. Toomey. "That is, of course, if we are not imposing on your good man here."

That night Dalton decided to retire early, while Toomey continued the discussions with Mr. Benton. The boys were hustled off to bed early, too, so they didn't know just when Dr. Toomey was escorted to his quarters over the store. All they knew was what they heard the next morning before they had a chance to get to breakfast.

"That man is something of a maniac!" Toomey was saying. "Do you know that he sleeps with a loaded revolver under his pillow?"

"Well, he has never shown a violent side to me," Benton reassured him, with all the conviction he could muster.

"It's not that it's any of my business," Toomey continued, "but I think you might be interested to know that your man is circulating tracts printed by the Russelite sect."

Toomey was both irascible and exhausted from lack of sleep. Bill Benton was mostly astonished. He was not so concerned that Dalton might be a Russelite, but he wondered what possessed him to sleep with a revolver under his pillow, most likely the same gun that was kept in the drawer downstairs near the safe.

More conversations took place after the kitchen door was closed. But later, after the horse had been harnessed at the stable, and after Toomey had driven on up the road, Benton called his cousin into the stock room. Some loud talk could be heard, but it dropped to a lower register and finally a ripple of laughter could be heard as they emerged into the open store.

"Maybe you don't like preachers, Dalt, but you don't have to scare them out of their wits," the boys heard their father say.

Dalton had been appeased, but he was still smouldering. Finally he fumed up temporarily and then let everything go in the interests of future understanding. "Bill," he affirmed, "if ever another one of those wandering penguins is thrown into my igloo, you can say goodbye to your star salesman."

Bill Benton just smiled. "Just put that shootin' iron back in the drawer where it belongs," he said. "In future we'll just have to find another place for the Lord's workers when they come this way." The Benton lads disappeared through the delivery entrance in the stock room in silent admiration for their pop.

Late that afternoon, Gordon Didgey called the three Benton boys outside to see something *of extreme urgency*. It was a big brown envelope that he had just received in the mail, marked *RUSH*.

There was an abandoned wagon-box lying in the deep grass on a vacant lot across the street from the store—an ideal summer headquarters for secret meetings of the juvenile brotherhood. The box had been sitting there so long that it blended into the landscape, and it was now so rickety and sun-bleached that the *ADAMS* trademark showed only as a misty green outline.

To come from the Gold Medal People and be marked *RUSH* like that, must sure mean that it was important. "And it sure shows what they must think of Gordon Didgey," Jamie said as they scrambled into the open end of the old derelict.

Gordon knew what was inside the envelope because he had felt impelled to open it before. So he spread everything out on the ground before them without saying a word. There it was—the finest array of boxing gloves, bicycles and cowboy belts—a glossy array of magic devices, adventure books and all of the fancy paraphernalia any kid would want to transport him to imaginative glory.

"An' all you have to sell is some Ferry Berries or something to men who want to keep their breath 'intimately fresh', and some kind of bottled stuff called My Sin Lotion for ladies who want to 'thrill like mad'." Gordon was enthusiastic as he read some of the more pertinent passages from the literature.

"That would be the first pair of boxing gloves in Quagmire!" Norman observed, as if he had just stumbled upon some great truth.

"They sure sound like powerful potions, if we can think of who needs them here in Quagmire," added young Bobby, as he devoured the coloured pictures with eager eyes. Rip Hogan and those guys at the livery stable all chewed plug tobacco or Copenhagen snuff and should all be prospective customers for Ferry Berries, they thought. Nobody knew anybody who wanted to "thrill like mad," but some nice ladies like Mrs. Kowalchuck might want some stuff to pour on their babies' bottoms or something. Even ol' Dalt could use some of those Ferry Berries to clean out his mouth after saying such rotten things as he did about "the penguin."

And again they were back on the subject of evil.

Every time they wanted to do something, did that subject have to come up? Did ol' Dalt think he had to stand guard over the candy pails because he was mean, or was it because he had some divine appointment to defend the Ten Commandments?

These thoughts were running through the minds of the wagon-box conferees when their attention strangely shifted to the space left by a missing board from the west side of the box. Through it they could see the store front in full perspective.

Gordon Didgey had learned a lot of tricks when he had lived in the Cape Breton mining town, and he liked to demonstrate to the prairie kids whenever the opportunity should arise. As he reached into a rear pocket to bring out a fragment of broken mirror, he remarked in the manner of an amateur sage, "Tempt not the forces of evil, for they will reveal their venom"—words he remembered from a cartoon strip.

Holding the mirror up to the sun's rays, he picked up a bright beam, reflected it back across the street and right into ol' Dalt's eyes.

At first he raised an arm to protect his vision, then shifted position to avoid the aggravation. The beam followed him. But nobody realized that the source of the annoyance could be traced.

Dalton swung the doors open and scrambled down the steps as fast as his short legs could carry him. Realizing instantly that they might be trapped like a bunch of mice in an oat bin, the tricksters bailed out of their nest in utter confusion, heading into the back alley and toward the first refuge that seemed to hold promise of safety—Rip Hogan's livery barn.

Ducking under a hanging door, they skirted a pile of fresh manure and mounted a ladder that led up into the haymow. The steps creaked and bits of chaff and straw tumbled back into their faces as they mounted upward.

It was quiet up there. Stacks of hay and straw were piled about—great places to hide if the pursuit continued. Openings in the floor along the walls led to chutes to the stalls below. A slip into one of these might end up in a horse manger down in the barn, so they were given a wide berth. All was silent again. They knew they had out-foxed their pursuer. He hadn't been able to squeeze under the door, and he wouldn't want to get his shoes all fouled with manure in any case. They felt safe.

As they gazed about through the dim shadows in the loft, it seemed as if they were in another world. Shafts of light entered only through two small windows high on the front wall, and through the cracks between ill-fitting boards. Pigeons in the rafters puffed their chests and made "chit-a-coo" sounds at one another. Gordon said they sounded like they were gargling spit. Huge cobwebs hung like dirty laundry laden with dust, chaff and the wings of dead flies. But, through it all, the perfume of the new hay permeated the place in a grand struggle to overpower the smells of sweaty horses and musty bedding straw.

Up near the front to the left, the sound of men's voices could be heard, muffled by the sound of shifting feet in the horse stalls and the munching of grain. Downstairs, no doubt, was where they had tied the tin cans on Pomroy's bull; and this was the haymow where, according to Tuffy Parsons, harvesters off the freights sometimes went to take a bath. It seemed that strangers from Ontario and Quebec came on the fall excursions and Rip Hogan discovered he could make ten cents a fill to provide wash water in a big tub in the mow.

"Tuffy Parsons told me that once there were some floozies up here, too," revealed the well-informed little Jamie.

"Maybe that is the kind of sin the Reverend Gow was talking about," Norman added, although he had no immediate suggestion as to how it might be rooted out.

Gordon Didgey had just found a grey cat with a bunch of kittens in the corner of the mow, when Bobby beckoned to him from the front. He crept forward as silently as possible. There was a screened-over vent in the floor and this was where the sound of voices was coming from. They could look down and actually see the men talking, joking and sending up clouds of tobacco smoke.

Somebody was saying something about the Quagmire Mixing

Station, wondering who was going to get the job of mixing grasshopper poison for the new crop year.

"He'll have to be a Liberal, to be able to make that stuff," ol' Rip Hogan remarked as he dislodged a wad of tobacco from under his lip.

"That won't be no problem fer Uncle Herman," young Hooley volunteered. "He'd take a job nuttin' jack rabbits fer the Bolsheviks if his ol' woman snapped her fingers."

But ol' Rip had no time to get into these conversations. He was putting special attention to an egg in the palm of his hand. He held it firm and dipped a small brush into a sardine can containing some sort of liquid. The shell of the hen's egg was brown, but where he was applying the liquid it was turning a few shades lighter.

"That should fix those silly buggers," he said as he viewed his masterpiece.

"What are you usin' there fer acid, Rip—vinegar or horse piss?" asked Rafe Pinder, followed by some hearty guffaws.

Rip affirmed that he was using vinegar, and showed how he could take the brown pigment right out of the shell by working over the same surface with the brush for some time. The numbers "1933" were appearing quite distinctly in a light milky shade.

"I've listened to them damned Russelites yappin' about the end of the world comin' in 1933 fer so long that I don't figger to take it any longer. I've decided to just give Armageddon a little help," he said with a whiskery grin. "Ye know that there Maude Abernethy with the backside on 'er like a German zeppelin? She keeps leavin' her damned pamphlets around here every time she gits to town, an if you don't listen she gits all worked up like she was churnin' butter an' a mouse hopped into the cream. It's time her hens got to givin' her a hand in revealin' the scriptures. Maybe she'd let up a spell."

With that, he held his artwork aloft for all to see. "Jim," he said, "as soon as she gits dark tonight, an all that Abernethy aggregation gits bedded down fer the night, I want you to slip down the tracks to their farm, sneak into the henhouse someways an put this here 'bible prophesy egg' into one of the nests along with a couple other deng good white ones. I'd do 'er meself, but I can't run as fast these days as I used to."

Norman looked at Bobby and they both looked at Gordon Didgey. Although they had been as silent as ghosts, their minds had been churning out a mess of questions. Was this the sort of evil Miss Keatch had to fight in India? Was Rip Hogan sitting there doing the work of Satan before their very eyes? Were the forces of righteousness marching to glory on the side of Bill Benton and Dr. Toomey, or with ol' Dalt and Maude Abernethy? Were they bearing witness to a bona fide sin in the making?

Those were all pressing questions that needed to be discussed. But not here. First, they must make a strategic withdrawal from the haymow and get to safer territory—away from the scene of the evil-doing.

For a full thirty-six hours, a great calm seemed to settle over the village and its environs. Wednesday morning came. Black smoke from the blacksmith's forge announced to all and sundry that Jerry Culligan was on the job and ready for the day's work. Singly and in teams, horses from the livery stable were brought to the watering trough while the gasoline engine chugged and banged away to keep the water spilling from the rusty iron pump into the troughs.

The first rig in town was a light wagon drawn by a pair of mules. The driver didn't even stop. Then, about nine o'clock, as the heat of the day commenced to be felt, a two-horse rig came up over the hill from the east, the driver standing up waving his hands and the team running at full gallop.

Frank Abernethy had both hands on the reins. Portly Maude squatted beside him with one hand clutching her Sunday hat and the other anchored to the railing along the side of the seat. They rounded the corner near the horse trough on two wheels and drew up at the hitching-post in front of the Benton store with a flourish that died in a puff of dust.

Frank tossed his reins to the ground, leaped out after them and looped the haltershank fast to the post. The morning breeze carried the sweet smell of wet leather and lathered flanks.

When Maude had gained her composure sufficiently to straighten her dress and pat out a rumpled collar, she reached for Frank's outstretched hand and tumbled her considerable bulk to the ground in a flair of white petticoats.

By this time the whole village had picked up the excitement, and people started to appear from everywhere. Some extraordinary news was about to break and nobody in Quagmire was going to miss out. Bill Benton appeared on the front steps of the general store in his butcher's apron; Mrs. Pinder still had twisters in her hair; Jerry Culligan and Lignite Joe came over from the blacksmith shop; and there was a full complement of Quagmire kids plus some out-of-towners visiting the Parsons. Three men came out from the Searle Elevator, and you could hear a dull clang at the lumber yard as the gate ran shut. It was reminiscent of the morning the Jepsen kid fell in the well. Everybody was there, including Rafe Pinder, Young Hooley and Rip Hogan from the livery stable.

Maude took up her position as the crowd moved in closer.

"May the glory of the Lord Jehovah God be with the people of Quagmire this day," she began, with billowy arms lifted skyward. "For this is the day of Revelation! The Day of Armageddon is at hand and the coming of the Kingdom is near." Her voice was rising in pitch and her flushed cheeks had taken fire.

"As we gather around this here hitchin' post, the eyes of Jehovah are upon the righteous and the unrighteous alike. Woe to the scribes, Pharisees, hypocrites and sinners who will not repent now," she gushed forth. "Youze have had yer chance, cause I've told yez a thousand times. But now there's only a little time left to deliver yerselves from calumny and destruction."

Many people could not quite understand what she was getting at yet, but her voice rose in strength and pent-up thoughts poured forth like a mud dam that had burst back in the coulee.

"Give us a sign, we asked the Lord last Friday. He didn't wait long, fer Frank and me now has the answer. His ears were listening to our supplications 'cause last night a message from Heaven was delivered in our henhouse. Yes! To our lowly place right there at the correction line, on section forty-two, near the gravel pit. It was a divine witness."

That made them take notice. Mrs. Pinder was standing next to Bobby and his friends. Even his uncle Dalt had arrived, smiled and put his hand on Bob's head. By this time Toby, their brindle collie, had found them in the crowd and was licking any hand that was extended to greet him. But all eyes were solidly glued on Mrs. Abernethy.

"Like the dew of Herman that descendeth upon the mountains of Zion, the truth of salvation shall spread through these here coulees," Maude continued to orate, with love and joy emanating from her eyes.

"The dew of Herman?" pondered Gordon Didgey in puzzlement. "Isn't that the guy that's trying to get the job over at the grasshopper mixing station?"

"Herman hasn't got enough dew to dampen down one batch of mash," ol' Rip Hogan interjected, and Rafe Pinder followed up with, "Will the Liberals be passin' out favours in the Promised Land?"

Maude Abernethy was not to be tampered with, though. This was her mission of revelation and she was not going to be distracted by such creatures of wrong-doing as Rafe Pinder and Rip Hogan. She hit them with the hardest broadside that would come to her tortured mind.

"Neither idolators, nor adulterers, nor fornicators shall have everlasting life, and them that is redeemed shall live in eternal glory," she bellowed in their direction.

Whatever that meant to the general gathering would be hard to know, but it certainly straightened out the distractors. Rip put his cap back on his head and pulled the peak down over his face with a grin. Gordon Didgey gave Norman a nudge, for the quartet were doing their best to stifle a snicker.

"Now, friends of Quagmire," Maude continued, "a dread judgement is on the wind—worse than drought, saw-fly, sow thistle, rusty wheat, hail storms or German measles. And them as has defiled the marriage bed have the worst drubbin' of all in store. But we still have time—precious time—as has been revealed in this revelation."

With these words she swung around and motioned to Frank, standing ready at the side of the wagon. He carried forward a fancy box filled to the brim with white goose down and skirted daintily with the frilliest of lace. In the centre, radiant in its setting, was a deep-brown hen's egg, upon whose surface was inscribed the unmistakable numerals "1933"—the predicted end of the world. The numbers were faint, but in the bright sunlight, they were visible from ten feet.

The Benton boys stood still, looking at the ground in order not to betray any signs of amusement. But, to the crowd, the message which the egg conveyed was not in question. Maude Abernethy smiled as blandly as though her chocolate cake had won the red ribbon at Moose Jaw Fair.

After everybody had had a chance to view the "portent" at close range, the general gathering divided into little islands of discussion. Frank stood guard so that nobody would get close enough to cause an accident. "Arrangements," he said, "should be made so that people in all parts of Saskatchewan, at least, can see the omen and prophesy with their own eyes." Mrs. Pinder thought somebody should contact the *Regina Leader* without delay.

As the crowd milled around, the men from the livery stable decided it was an opportune moment to make their exit. The Benton boys and Gordon Didgey watched them as they disappeared around the corner leading to the pool hall. Young Hooley slapped ol' Rip on the back so firmly it nearly knocked him over. Rafe Pinder was doubled over and holding his sides. The crowd was so entranced with the "Abernethy find" that the culprits disappeared unnoticed. Mission accomplished.

When emotions had settled down somewhat, and many had gone home, Maude had a serious conversation with Bill Benton. She said something about the "coming order of righteousness" and the "blameless upright life," and Benton assured her that he would be pleased to donate some space in his show windows so more people of the community could view "the great omen," pending some decision about its eventual resting place. He said that he would make sure that no harm would come to it because cousin Dalt would be put in full charge of security.

So, that is just where it rested for the ensuing days—right between a pyramid of Aunt Jemima's Pancake Flour and some bags of Sure Gain Chick Feed.

That night the boys had another meeting in the wagon-box to discuss the day's events. Dalt saw them go there with some other kids in tow and appeared immediately with chocolate bars for everybody. He said that it had been a memorable day, one long to be remembered. He also said that, for some, the best was yet to come.

After he had gone, the discussion delved into a good many aspects of this strange thing called sin. Gordon Didgey suggested that what Rip Hogan had done was possibly a "Holy Sin." On this they agreed, because Gordon Didgey was a smart cookie.

Little Jamie wondered what angle of the prophesy would be fulfilled if the egg sat in the warm sun long enough and hatched—right next to the chick feed, too.

4

THE RELUCTANT CAPITALISTS

MIKE Symboluk, section foreman on the C.P.R. right-of-way leading out of Quagmire, had a crew of six Galicians working for him, and they kept the rails in tip-top running order for six miles on either side of the three elevators. That was a big responsibility, and though he "broke talk" (as he said) with his English, most of the younger boys of the village liked him because he encouraged them to visit the bunkhouses in off-hours.

That was one reason why young Punk Jordan suddenly asked one day if anyone knew whether or not Mike had got his wife shipped over from the Old Country yet.

It was Sunday afternoon and the sun was beaming hot. Norman and Bob Benton, Gordon Didgey and Punk sat beside the blacksmith shop chewing plug licorice. Punk whittled on his new slingshot and Toby lay sprawled in the grass with his tongue spilling out on the ground. Punk had introduced the subject of the Galicians mostly because he was bored listening to others talk about business.

Gordon had the agency for the Gold Medal People, but hadn't sold any My Sin perfume or Ferry Berries to men with stinky breath. The men at the livery barn who chawed plug tobacco didn't seem to care much about offending anybody.

"Why does everybody always want to have us selling something when it's summer holidays?" said Bobby.

Just yesterday, a fancy dude of a traveller in the Benton store had wanted his dad to take on the agency for Sequoia made-to-measure pants. Benton said he didn't have time to bother, so the traveller had talked to Norman about it. He said that Sequoia cloth was a new invention that would "wear like a pig's nose." All Norman had to do was become a "tapeman for Sequoia," and he'd make more money than the harvesters stooking wheat or the Galicians shoveling gravel and tamping ties along the railbed.

"And what," Norman said, "does that guy know about how much the Galicians got paid for working the C.P.R.?"

The boys didn't know, either, but they knew most of the section hands at Quagmire and were glad to go with them for rides on the jigger. Some days they would go up past the trestle and explore the coulees all day until the work-day was finished. Toby was allowed to ride, too, and that was pretty terrific.

Mike Symboluk's wife had not arrived yet. Louisa Benton would have known, because she had helped him send the papers to the immigration office. So the four boys got to their feet, sauntered across the road to the weigh-scales, and then down the cutbank where three converted boxcars stood on the siding.

The door of the second car was ajar and someone could be heard picking out a tune on a mandolin. Mike Symboluk, Steve Kakarovich and Peter Kalinka were the ones Norman and Bob knew best because they were grocery customers at the Benton store. Bill Benton could never understand what they did with all the cabbage, beans and sowbelly they bought, but his boys saw the slabs of sandwiches and the pots of soup and bottles of ketchup that disappeared at mealtimes. It wasn't much of a mystery to them.

There were no women cooks around because, as they said, they were all waiting in the Old Country for funds to arrive so they could emigrate. There were no children. They sang songs in languages the boys could not understand—Ukrainian, Polish, Hungarian or Russian—which confused and bewildered most of the farm people around Quagmire. To make it simpler, the locals just called them all Galicians and that was all there was to it.

At the door of the bunkhouse where the music was coming from, Mike Symboluk, the foreman, stuck his head out, and his leathered face broke into a whiskery grin.

"Yok sha myish, boys, welcome to Bessarabia," were his words of greeting. "You forget to show passports when you approach to Royal

C.P.R. Embassy,'' he chuckled.

Boisterous laughter erupted inside as the boys climbed the short iron ladder. As on previous occasions, some men were sitting around a card table. Pete Kalinka was getting a haircut in the middle of the room, and another fellow was reading a paper with printing that Bobby said "looked like turkey tracks in soft mud.''

Though the cookhouse was located in the next car, it seemed that everybody was congregated in the central bunkhouse. Beds were made up, but socks and underwear hung from a two-by-four railing across the front of the bunks, and shirts hung over the end-posts. Steve Kakarovich wore fleece-lined drawers all year round, so the boys knew where he slept. There was an Eaton's catalogue lying open on the floor with some other scattered papers that Punk Jordan was already snooping through.

"Here's your old grade two reader,'' he said with surprise, picking up a tattered book and showing Norman his name scrawled over the inner cover.

Norman knew that his mother had given it to Mike Symboluk one night when he was buying groceries. He wanted to learn to read English, so Louisa Benton had given him the reader for practice.

"I am Rax, ze pat fox. I have a box weeth a rog in eet to sit upon,'' mocked Peter Kalinka.

Mike looked sheepish for the moment when he realized his reading was being ridiculed, but then he laughed, banged the table and said with a broad smile, "You crazzy buggar guys! Som time you laugh like sick cow when you see Mike Symboluk beeg shit politician in Regina Govermint!''

The card game resumed. Gordon Didgey was talking to the dark man sitting on the couch. The Benton lads thought they should get acquainted, too, but as they began to move in his direction, they caught sight of a single sheet of writing paper lying on the floor. It was beginning to move, literally walking its way from the couch to the apple box in the other corner of the room.

"You come to talk to Houdini, zee great Hungarian magician?'' he asked out of the corner of his mouth. "My name is Fedor,'' he continued. "I am not Houdini but I show you magic treek.'' With that his arm dropped and a shower of coins spilled to the floor.

"Kind of clumsy magician,'' remarked little Jamie. "But is this your writing paper on the floor?''

With that, Gordon Didgey swooped down, picked up the sheet and turned it over. On the underside was a housefly with its wings stuck fast to the paper and its feet flailing the air in an effort to get traction.

Well, it might have been a novel idea to employ fly-power in order to create this illusion, but possibly Fedor had other and deeper motivations—just to make contact with the younger fry, an association that he needed and missed.

Meanwhile, the man in the upper bunk who was plucking a few familiar chords on the mandolin, suddenly broke into an exciting polka.

The small bunkhouse filled quickly with the music. The card game stalled because there were no hands left on the table. They were in the air keeping time to the lilt and sway of the tune, with hobnailed boots brushing on the floor.

"Krakowiak ees name of dees polka," Steve whispered into Gordon's ear. "I am hearink it dees song first time in Krakov, mine home place in Poland. Now ees come to Canada. You like?"

Gordon did, for he was also drawn into the flood of nostalgia that was being unleashed. Norman was explaining to his younger brothers that, in Europe, ladies with long silk gowns danced to this kind of music in lavish crystal ballrooms and he had no doubt that Steve Kakarovich had been a part of it all. Possibly, he thought, there might someday be one of those ballrooms built near the community hall in Quagmire. But enough of the dreaming. The mandolin slowed the pace into a Mazurka. A note of sadness seemed to settle, and everybody went back to playing cards.

Frank Kupinski went to the drawer to get cigarette papers and a tobacco pouch, hand tooled as a gift. He did not return for some time, but remained fully engrossed in a photograph tacked to the wall over his bunk. It was a picture of a rather stout lady and two girls of school age.

Another man had sat in the chair in the centre of the room and was getting a haircut. Black, grey and brown clippings were now mingled together on the floor, and Gordon Didgey noted that the shorn heads were all rounder than the heads that came out of Pinder's Barber Shop over town. Mike Symboluk had such a short neck that two folds ran full across the back before it fitted into his collar. "It must be him that eats all that fat pork," Jamie was heard to comment.

Well, it seemed that even the thought of food around that place had its results, for about that time Kazimir appeared in the doorway. He was from the cookhouse next door, and he was toting a big kettle of victuals. The boys didn't know his last name, but they knew his reputation. Plates, cups, spoons and knives were passed to everybody, and the boys were invited to take all of the holubchi they could handle. Cabbage rolls packed with meat and rice, and seasoned with chili sauce or some other flavorous potion—tastes of the Slavic homeland and of the steppes of Asia, right there on the C.P.R. siding at Quagmire. And another thing the boys found liberating—they could drink tea with the men without restriction.

"How you like dees holubchi, boy?" asked Kazimir, putting a gnarled hand on Bob's head. "I buy kapusta from your daddy' store. He good man. Me no money, you' daddy geev cradit." Bill Benton cashed all pay cheques, the C.P.R. was as solid as a marlin spike, and credit was available to anyone with calloused hands.

But the mere mention of their father suddenly reminded the Bentons that they had ties at home. A clock on the wall informed them that it was now going on six o'clock—supper time, and their stomachs already full. The boys concluded that they must go home. But there was one item of business which they had come to discuss in the first place and were certainly not going to forget now. How about tomorrow? It was still summer holidays, and could they go out with the section hands on the jigger?

"I tal you, boy. Maybe you makit me trobble," said Mike, "but you come anyway." Mike was the section foreman and he made the decisions. "Soon's commink school-time. You stoddy an make smart keeds but tomorrow you makit fon an chase jack rabbit and gophers."

"Duja dobra," Bobby answered, expending his entire Ukrainian vocabulary. "We'll be at the grain elevators in the morning when you pass."

The next morning at 7:30, the three Bentons, Gordon Didgey and one dog stood waiting at the siding where the switches diverted freight cars to the grain elevators. As usual, Punk Jordon had slept in again. The Bentons had lunches packed in a brown paper bag and Norman was in charge of the twenty-two calibre rifle. Bill Benton had also given them a package of fifty shells with the understanding that they should bring back twenty-five gopher tails to be redeemed for two cents each at the municipal office. With this kind of marksmanship they could collect fifty cents, pay for the shells, and have twenty-five cents spending money. Benton was convinced that such an arrangement would teach his boys to be thrifty and at the same time help the farmers to protect the wheat crop from the pesky rodents. Louisa Benton set down her own supplementary rules—only fire at stationary objects and never in the direction of somebody's cows.

Only a few minutes had passed before they could hear the jigger rolling along the tracks with the gasoline engine barking out a sharp abuse upon the stillness of the morning air. At the closed switch, it came to a squealing stop.

To some people, these vehicles were called "speeders" because they had a motor and could attain a relatively high speed, but to the younger set they were all "jiggers." Mike was the one who looked after the throttle, so Steve Kakarovich saw his immediate role as conductor in charge of passengers. "Have it your teekits raddy, boys," he announced. "Next train two hours late an' cost dobble."

"Double times nothin' is nothin'," Gordon Didgey reminded him, scrambling aboard, while Norman and Bobby lifted Toby up at the front.

"Dees passenger—no suitcase—go to obserwation deck," said Mike, grinning as he hoisted the dog up to the platform over the engine. He had ridden there before and was obviously looking forward to riding into the wind with his nose acting as a jib and his two shaggy ears blowing back in the wind.

Two miles down the track they noticed Elmer Woothey patching a gate. It looked as though his horses had been trying to break out. Then the jigger was crossing the high wooden trestle, past barrels of water sitting out on their platforms and making clumping noises at every joint in the rails. It was quite a thrill to look down over the edge far into the coulee below as the wooden girders creaked like ghosts with rheumatism. Then an echo would come back up through the criss-cross of timbers, as if the sound had become lost. Norman and his little brother sat close together holding onto Toby's tail. Gordon Didgey said they had bigger bridges in Cape Breton.

Another two or three miles down the tracks, the road-bed curved to the left, leading to a second but lower trestle. The jigger came to a squealing stop. This was destination for the day—the place where some work would be done tamping ties and removing weeds from the right-of-way.

Here the coulee emptied out into a wide alkali flat and the crop was thin in the adjacent fields. Two red-tailed hawks hovered over the bulrushes where the creek widened and disappeared into the bog. There was ample opportunity to explore the sedges and some muskrat huts in the vicinity, and there was a deserted coal mine in the side of the hill that warranted some investigation. But, best of all, gophers scurried about, sitting up like little pegs driven into the ground. The boys scrambled down off the jigger, and the crew lifted it off the tracks to a knoll where it would be out of the way when the "two-forty-five" came through from Weyburn.

The hours passed quickly that day. Most of the morning was spent in and around the rank stands of bulrushes. There they found a dilapidated raft that had been thrown together from discarded railroad ties by someone during the hunting season. This was good for a re-enactment of Mutiny on the Bounty. When the noon hour rolled around, they found shade by an old wall made from fieldstones, an ideal place for lunch. By three o'clock there were only three .22-bullets left for the rifle and the count of gopher tails was satisfactory. Everybody was happy but the gophers. Even Toby, though he had spoiled some good shots by running in wide circles like a fool possessed and digging furiously into holes where there was no chance of finding anything at home.

The little band of adventurers was giving some serious thought to entering the old mine shaft to see if there was any coal left, when they heard Mike calling them to go. The work day was over, the jigger had been pushed up to the tracks, and the men were wiping the sweat and grime off their tanned bodies so that shirts could be hauled over their heads. It must have been a hotter day on the tracks than down in the coulee, because Steve Kakarovich looked like a badger with typhoid fever standing there with stringy wet hair standing up in all directions.

The front end of the jigger was being lifted off the ground in the first move to get it back on the rails when the ear-splitting shriek of a train whistle shattered the quiet country air. Up ahead, an engine was coming down through the draw. It was pulling only three cars, but sending billows of black smoke into the heavens.

The "two-forty-five" express had gone through on time. There was no scheduled traffic until a freight due at about seven-fifteen that evening. What was this?

Mike Symboluk looked up with a start and leaped back to a position of safety. The section gang scattered as the engine roared and clattered and split the air with another piercing scream. The coal-tender passed, then a coal car and finally an observation coach with open platform at the rear fitted with a brass railing that glistened in the sun. One man, dressed in a light suit and Panama hat, stood at the rail while he smoked a long black cigar and spoke with another person seated in the lounge chair backed up to the car wall.

As the whistle again emitted a short blast, a big jack rabbit jumped up from behind a clump of Russian thistle and went bounding off over the field as though he was riding on a set of newly tempered springs. But he wasn't nearly as disturbed as Steve Kakarovich. He threw his C.P.R. shovel crashing to the ground, ran his sausage-shaped fingers through his tousled hair and set off striding down the tracks shaking his fist aloft and screaming at the top of his lung capacity, "GOD

DAMNED CA-PA-TA-LEESTIC SON A GO BEECH!!!''

Mike Symboluk just mumbled to himself. The boys looked on in puzzled bewilderment. Steve was all wet, and red, and mad, and looked as wild as the spooky mustang they had watched Jerry Culligan try to put shoes on at the blacksmith shop last week.

"I tal you meester," he fumed, "all dees bastard capataleest dogs should bego to Siberia."

"Or maybe Sask-at-u-onski?" quipped Fedor.

Mike Symboluk kept cool, as befitted the position of section foreman, but he was mad, too. "Eef train come ten minoot later, we all be dad," he said to Gordon Didgey, his big craggy hand spanning his face.

During the ride home nobody said much. When they arrived at the Benton store, there was little dialogue, either. If the truth was told at home, there was a chance that mother and father Benton might want to clamp down on such outings with the Galicians. But the boys had a meeting again that night in the old wagon-box on the vacant lot.

"What is a *capitaleest*, I wonder?" Gordon Didgey pondered.

Nobody had any idea, but they suspected that it must be an ogre of some kind. Were the men in the white suits acting that way on purpose? Didn't they care if they smashed the jigger and all the people that were on it? Why hadn't someone let Mike know they were coming? Or didn't they care? It all seemed such a mixed-up affair that nothing was decided. There was nothing to do but go home and go to bed.

But sleep does not come easily to minds that are in turmoil. After everything had gone dark in the room, Bobby considered discussing it further under the blankets with Jamie. But what was the use? What did he know about men wearing fancy suits and Panama hats?

He drifted off to sleep, but it was a fitful rest. There are those particular kinds of sleep where a boy can imagine that someone outside his body is getting into his brain-box and stirring everything up with a big porridge spoon. It is possible to doze into some kind of comfortable slumber, then a thought comes racing in from some extraneous wilderness and contradicts everything that has hitherto been settled and concluded. Sometimes one can even get to the point that it is difficult to determine whether strange sounds are part of a dream or are actually happening in the real world.

And this was the case when the distant sound of a train whistle seemed to penetrate the gloom of Bobby's bedroom. The message was repeated in short blasts. This, he knew, was the C.P.R. language of distress.

In a moment he was wide awake and standing beside his bed. His suspicions were reinforced when he became conscious of the fact that Norman, who slept in the adjacent bed, was also awake and now tugging on his blanket.

"Git up!!! Something is going on down on the railway tracks. Sounds like maybe some kind of accident. Let's get our bikes and sneak down the side road in the dark, so's maybe we kin be witnesses," he whispered.

"What time is it?" Bobby asked, wondering how much more time there was 'til daybreak.

"It's three o'clock. I heard the kitchen clock. But we want it dark and the moon is just right."

Pants and shirts were hurriedly drawn on, and down the stairs they crept without taking time even to look again. In ten minutes they were peddling steadily in the direction of the first trestle.

Half a mile down the road, they heard the engine let out a series of powerful chugs that diminished into shorter belches of steam. The piston had been engaged and the boys knew that the train was now in motion. They wheeled their bikes into the ditch, lay flat against its vertical edge and watched through the page-wire fence as the freight cars rattled past.

"Remember where we saw Mr. Woothey fixing his gate yesterday?" Norman queried. "There's some horses running loose in the field there and some people herding them back along the fence line toward his buildings. We have to wait a little longer."

Bobby was wondering if the "capitalists" had something to do with what was going on. "They're gone now," he said. "Let's leave our bikes here and move up a little closer."

As they made their way up in the dark, the forms of three horses could be recognized lying sprawled over the cinders at the side of the track and another down on the side of the grade in the grass. They appeared to be very dead.

Creeping up in the gloom, they found the bodies to be two bay mares, a white-faced roan gelding and a dappled grey colt—all glassy-eyed and terribly gashed. Residues of clotted blood left red blotches where the remainder had soaked away through the cinders.

"If the capitalists did it, I wonder if they are going to come back?" Bobby questioned. "They didn't let Mike know when they were running their train yesterday, so they can come any time they want, I guess."

"Dead horses won't be much use to anyone," Norman replied with the wisdom of his additional two years. "And they won't likely be much good to Mr. Woothey now, either."

The two Benton lads poked around and looked at the horses more closely. One was lying with part of its tail across the rail.

"Horsehair!!" Norman exclaimed. "Do you know what we can get for that from the Northwest Hide and Fur Company? Forty cents a pound. There was a price list came jist last week. Don't ya remember where we sent the weasel skins last winter?"

"Gee! That's better than sellin' Sequoia made-to-measure pants," Bobby enthused.

And, as if by sibling telepathy, both kids had the same idea at the same time. Back to the bikes, and back home for some gunny sacks and some scissors. There was no time to be wasted, because in an hour the sun would be up.

"If they see us, somebody might think *we* killed the horses," Bobby gasped, pushing his pedals at top capacity.

By the time they got home, collected the necessary gear and returned to the scene of the accident, the gloom of early morning was hanging like a pall on the earth.

Norman cut off the tail hair while Bobby was busy on the manes, both hurriedly stuffing their bags to the brim. Toby looked on, but he just curled his lip and whimpered. He seemed to be relieved when the bags were tied and carried back over the ditch to the waiting bikes.

"This ain't stealin', is it?" asked Bobby.

"Only if the horses are alive," came the unqualified reply.

When they wheeled into the village, the sun was just sending its first shafts of light over the horizon. Nobody was around, so they took their loot to a small barn where the family cow was stabled. There it would stay until it had all been sorted out and packed for shipping. But, back to bed now, before Louisa Benton called everybody for breakfast.

In bed, however, little sleeping took place because there were still some serious things to think about. Should their father be told? How could the parcel be shipped without everybody in town knowing about it?

At the breakfast table, later on, the sound of the jigger could be heard making its daily trip to the working site. What would the Galicians think when they discovered four dead horses with fresh haircuts front and back?

That Tuesday, just after the Benton store opened at eight, Frank Jepson drove into town. The first thing he mentioned when he got inside the store was whether or not Bill Benton had heard about the accident. He didn't even wait for an answer before he continued, "I heard a train tootin' and makin' a commotion once in the night, but jist thought they was shuntin' grain cars in the yard an' went back to sleep," he began. "Woothey figgers that somebody must have been tamperin' with his fence and let some of his horses out on the tracks. Killed four of 'em! They's gonna be some 'officials' down later in the morning to make an inspection."

Nothing was said about tampering with hair, so Norman made a face at Bob and they both withdrew to the cow barn.

The two bags were still there, so they were moved to the loft and covered with hay.

About ten o'clock, an engine and caboose went through the village of Quagmire and stopped near the trestle. From their vantage point on the ramp of the Searle Elevator, the boys could see men walking around and talking with Mr. Woothey who came out from the farmhouse. An hour later, the engine and caboose returned up the line to Assiniboia. The boys had no way of knowing what was said. All they knew was that in the afternoon, the Galicians helped Mr. Woothey haul four carcasses off the right-of-way and into a deep ravine where they were covered with earth and stones. Norman explained to Bobby that it wouldn't be long before the coyotes found them. The coyotes wouldn't care whether or not the horses had full tails and manes.

The day passed; the next one dawned. Then another, and soon the week had passed without any news that could be called disturbing. Another week and school would be starting, so any unfinished business had to be cleared up as soon as possible. Plans had been made to buy some new baseball mitts and bats for the Weybridge team, and the sale of Sequoia pants and Ferry Berries had been a dismal failure.

Norman and Bobby were thinking about this on Saturday when they went to the cow barn again with a supply of string, a big darning needle and two address tags made out to the Northwest Hide and Fur Company of Winnipeg.

Wads of horsehair were packed into the gunny sacks as tightly as possible. The ends were folded in and sewed so generously with blue string that Bobby was reminded of the varicose veins on Mrs. Rasmusson's legs. When the tags were securely wired to the bundles, they were strapped onto the waiting bicycles and transported directly to the express office at the C.P.R. station.

The big problem was that Gordon Didgey's father was the station agent who weighed in the express bundles. Did they have to "declare the contents"? What commodities would two kids be shipping to the Northwest at this time of year? Cowhides, muskrat pelts, beaver castors, seneca root and a lot of such items were always on the price list, but "horsehair" somehow had a note of suspicion attached to it, particularly in light of recent events. But Norman and Bob sailed right up to the counter in the shipping room and hoisted up their parcel.

"Two bails of merchandise for shipment to Winnipeg," Norman announced. Bobby stood right back of him, filled with admiration.

Mr. Didgey looked out from under the blue celluloid visor he wore and opened his huge ledger to record the transaction.

"Consignor?" he asked. "Are you the shippers, that is?"

"You know what our names are, Mr. Didgey," Norman sang out and then stopped abruptly.

"Consignee?" the questioning continued. Nobody, evidently, had to answer that one, because he was copying the address down right off the tags.

"Nature of goods placed in transit?" It flowed off his tongue as natural as licorice-coloured spit, and then he stopped. "Been bumping off some cattle for their hides, or skinning some old range ponies or something?"

"Horsehair," blurted Norman. "We got lucky this summer. We're gonna buy some new baseball stuff fer school, an' Gordon is gonna be our pitcher." That should get to him, Bobby thought.

Mr. Didgey was writing "horsehair" in his big book when the door opened and in came Mike Symboluk and Steve Kakarovich. They were through work early on Saturdays and were just making some rounds on a visit.

"Horsehair," repeated Mr. Didgey, as though he was having difficulty with the spelling.

"Hello, boys," greeted their friends. "I see you make good beezness today. If I know you so good catch hair from horses, maybe we make partnership or start barbershop for broncos."

What he meant by that remark, the boys could hardly guess, but they didn't have to guess long. Suspicions on all sides were confirmed when they all broke down and started to laugh. They laughed as though the revolution was over and had succeeded.

"Beeg Quagmire mystery solved," announced Steve between snorts. "Such keeds I never see before—not even in Krakov!"

Well, the boys didn't know quite what to think or say. At least nobody seemed to be mad.

"We didn't steal the horsehair!" Bobby ventured.

"The capitalists likely killed the horses jist like they nearly killed you guys," bellowed Norman. "We jist wanted to save the horsehair so's they couldn't spoil it, too. They can make paintbrushes out of that stuff, you know!!"

"Ca-pa-ta-leestic sun a go beech! That's what I heard you call them yourself," Bobby hurled at Steve for good measure.

With that the laughing only got worse. Two more Galicians came through the door. There was some more talk in a strange language, and they laughed, too. One man said that, in Quagmire, the best "capita-leests" seemed to be the ones that regularly bummed rides on the C.P.R. jigger.

Two weeks later, a cheque for five dollars and eighty-two cents came in the mail from the Northwest Hide and Fur Company. It was delivered at the Quagmire post office, which was just back of the yardgoods counter in the Benton store.

5

DEUTERONOMY'S LAST STAND

*T*HE fragrance of ripening wheat was on the wind and the harvest was in full swing. Friday afternoon, when school was out, the Benton boys trudged the four miles back to Quagmire with more than the usual number of detours. Almost every threshing rig they passed was an excuse to loiter, if only to feel the hustle and excitement of the harvest season.

Possibly their favourite stop was the last one, where Jack Pomroy's big Rumley steam outfit sent clouds of dust and smoke into the air. Stook-wagons were coming to the separator with wobbly loads of bundles, in such a steady procession that the boys wondered if maybe some sort of signal system had been contrived and was transmitted by short whistle blasts. A shrill toot every once in awhile must mean something.

Bobby liked to stand behind the belching engine with his younger brother. It was a thrill to feel the earth shudder as the steam forced the big piston forward and back, setting the huge fly-wheel a-spinning while the rubber-covered belt ran out like a ribbon of blackstrap molasses. This, in turn, set the separator convulsing, sifting and shaking. Who knew what all went into its gaping maw, but straw, weed seeds and grain all came out like magic in separate places. Once some green farmhand had let a pitchfork fall into the revolving knives. Jamie wondered if something like that might happen some time when he was around.

The harvesters all wore bright polka-dot bandanas tight around their necks to keep chaff and dust from getting down into the hair on their chests. Jack's old striped cap with the puffy crown always sat half sideways on his bony head, and it was always wise to stand up-wind from him when he was chewing tobacco. Herman Hicks was the head spike-pitcher after having hung around the livery barn all summer, and it was obvious that he enjoyed the new title.

And the young fry watched with a fascinated gaze as the broad-rumped horses from the Jepson farm flattened out their haunches, strained at the tugs and pulled a brimming load of golden wheat out over the soft stubble field to the road and on to the grain elevators at Quagmire.

"That'll go number *ONE*-hard, surer 'en a hen eats grit," said ol' Jack as he scooped up a handful and let it run slowly through his fingers. "That Red Fife is sure a winner."

Sitting in the shade of the water-wagon was a full box of McIntosh apples, available to anyone who wanted one. Naturally, the boys dug in, because McIntosh reds were recognized as a once-a-year treat from the Okanagan Valley in B.C. Their tantalizing aroma somehow became closely associated with threshing machines.

At this time of year, the Benton store was a beehive of industry. Extra help was needed to put up the big orders of groceries going out to the farms to feed the hungry hordes of sun-tanned harvesters, many of whom came from the eastern provinces on excursion trains. Nobody paid cash at this time of year; it was "put 'er on the cuff 'til the crop is sold," and a grain cheque or two about Halloween time would settle the entire bill. There was no trouble with the farmers, but those harvesters from the East were another story. Mother Benton often explained to the boys that the men from Ontario were usually nice fellows in Ontario, but when they got west "there are some rough-necks among them." On Saturdays she often sent the lads back to the coulees for the day to get away from the "bad influence" and, of course, there would be Sunday School and church the following day to neutralize some of the high spirits.

It seemed to the kids that, at the weekend, when the chances of some fun with the harvesters were at their best, that the forces of sin got loose at the same time. It was that longstanding tug-of-war between evil influences that lurked at the pool hall and the livery stable aligned against the forces of decency.

After supper that Friday, Norman and Bobby went to call on Gordon Didgey. Punk Jordan was there, so the adventurers decided to get up early Saturday and spend the morning back in the hills near the clay pit. Maybe there would be some gooseberries left or some Saskatoons in the ravines that they could eat 'til they were really full without being told to stop.

After breakfast next morning, they gathered at the cowshed on the northern outskirts of the village. All four were barefoot as usual. Punk had a bandage on one toe, so they let him lead the way. Single file, they strung out down the slope to a long grade crossing the alkali flats.

Even the rocky hillside and the run-off ravine was a change from the flat emptiness that surrounded the townsite. Clumps of foxtail and yarrow brushed bare legs as they walked along, and even the grasshoppers and crickets were hard pressed to find cover in the dry grass. At intervals a gopher squeaked, giving away its whereabouts. A second gopher, standing bolt upright on his earthen mound, affording the widest possible vision, answered defiantly and then disappeared abruptly at the sight of a hovering chicken hawk. It seemed that all the creatures of the grasslands were out in search of food before the searing heat of the day.

Down along the side of the grade, ducks splashed around in the small ponds of water that had settled in the low spots. Bulrushes concealed rookeries of noisy terns and gabbling blackbirds. The troop of adventurers was following close along the water's edge, taunting the birds and checking on places where muskrats had burrowed into the bank, when they came upon the remains of a killdeer—just a few feathers, black and white, with the familiar band of white around the neck. "Some coyote or weasel has had breakfast there," remarked Gordon. The trek resumed.

Up to this time, the purpose of the entire expedition had no other motivation than to get four boys out of town. Sure, they were out for a hike, but to be a success every hike has to have some sort of focus.

The focus came when they started poking around some old abandoned farm buildings up in a draw just after the road left the alkali bottom. They were concealed from the road by a windbreak of neglected Russian poplars. Inside, the yard was overgrown with weeds. They didn't bother going near the house because the barn, with its door swinging half-open in the wind, was of greater interest—a real haven for bats, owls, mice, swallows and maybe the odd skunk.

Gordon Didgey was an accomplished snoop, so it didn't take long for him to get into all the bins and corners. Mouldy chaff, piles of rubbish that reeked of mouse nests, and a collection of hand implements with broken handles and missing parts were scattered about. Finally he came upon an old manure fork with two tines missing. He was poking it into the straw under one of the mangers when it dug into something a bit spongy. Blended with the musty smell of straw, the unmistakable odour of skunk wafted up into the open stall and permeated the barn.

In their uncluttered lives at Quagmire, opportunities like this, for the boys, did not present themselves very often. They had dreamed of capturing a live skunk many times.

"Ye know that ol' Lignite Joe that lives down in the coulee near the coal mine?" queried Gordon Didgey. "He catches skunks for their skins. I know, cause he brings them to my dad at the express office and sends them away."

"Don't they stink up the station and the express car on the train?" Punk Jordan asked.

"What do you think? They don't jist plunk 'em down on the counter with the stripes pointing toward Winnipeg, you nut!" Gordon answered indignantly. "They don't jist throw the skunk skins into the express car with the bread boxes and cream cans, either. They gotta have regulations, don't they? You have to bundle them tight in tarpaper, seal the ends and then wrap them again in brown paper. That's how they ship skunks without the stink!"

It was quite an impressive explanation, so Norman thought it was a good time to introduce the subject of capturing skunks alive.

"They can't spray you unless their back feet are flat on the ground. I read that in the Farmer's Almanac," he declared with an air of complete confidence.

Gordon Didgey did not believe that and had a smirk on his face. Bobby didn't like to see his big brother's credibility in question on this point, so he proceeded to add some vital information of his own. "He showed it to me, too. It was writ by a doctor for horses, and they know all about gizzards and glands and that stuff. He said that the stink comes from a gland that has some kind of a nipple inside the skunk's anus. And in case you don't know it, his anus is his ass-hole."

That was an observation of technical significance, so Norman was quick to carry the point even further.

"That's what they do," he said. "They put their feet flat on the ground, lift their tail over their backs so they can open up their anus. Then they spray with their nozzel an' fan the stinky stuff with their tail. If they can't git their feet down, they can't spray," he concluded with an air of finality.

Punk Jordan, a boy whose father had homesteaded in the Cypress Hills country, followed up this revelation with the confirming statement that he had once heard of an Indian picking up a skunk by the tail and throwing him into the Frenchman River so's the current would take him downstream into the camp of the Blackfeet.

With this kind of working knowledge at hand, why should they not take the skulking little critter under the manger into captivity and hold him for closer observation? It was just a matter of working out the details.

Out beyond the barn, Norman located a dilapidated crate that had been possibly used to keep a setting hen in when they didn't want her to go too broody. In quick order he removed a loose slat from the top and replaced it with a longer board that would protrude out at both ends. This could be fastened firmly with a nail at one end, and would swing wide at the other when they were ready to drop the captive through the opening. At that time the gap could be closed, the swinging end nailed down, and the result would be a portable cage with handles at either end for carrying. What a plan! They could hardly wait!

Gordon Didgey, the skeptic, picked up his old broken manure fork and again established contact with the animal in question. Norman stood in the manger with a length of buggy spring that he had scrounged from a trash pile. He was ready to pry the board loose directly above the skunk.

As the crack widened, a tuft of black hair mixed with white pushed through the opening. Norman was in a vulnerable position, so he instructed Bobby that when he pried the manger board wide open, Bobby was to grasp the black and white tail firmly. He was then to lift the skunk clear, carry him to the crate where Punk and Gordon would be waiting to close the lid and pound in the last nail.

If everything went according to plan, it would be just like in *The Boy's Own Annual* where Captain Witherspoon captured a wild boar in Tanganyika.

Well, Norman gave such a heave that the floorboard snapped in the middle. Bobby grasped the hairy tail and lifted the startled skunk directly into the open space, scattering sprigs of straw with his outstretched feet. Ten quick steps took him to the waiting crate. The horse doctor in the Almanac was right—there wasn't a whiff of perfume while the skunk was held aloft. But when he struck the bottom of the crate, the tail went directly back and the scene was something like the one at Punk Jordan's house, when his stupid sister forgot a can of sauerkraut she put in the oven.

Punk pounded his nail in as fast as he could. Everybody jumped back, and a cloud of yellow microscopic particles billowed up from the case. It was a wonder how the skunk could stand it himself.

It took fully fifteen minutes for everything to settle sufficiently so that the captors could move up close enough to inspect the cage. As adult skunks go, he was small, but he certainly registered big when it came to fumigating endowments.

So, with a prize like this in their possession, the next question posed itself. What should be the next logical move?

Well, in matters of this nature there are no logical answers. They would carry their prize back to Quagmire. There was no thought of where they might find lodgings; no thought of whether or not he would be a welcomed addition to the village; and no consideration of the fact that it was Saturday afternoon when throngs of farmers and harvesters would be everywhere.

As they retraced their route across the long grade, they found that the load would get heavy from time to time. It was necessary to sit down at intervals to rest. And it was during these stops that a feeling of harmony, even an empathy, began to grow between the boys and their furry captive. His wet nose and his inquiring beady eyes were enough in themselves, but his inquisitiveness seemed to have overcome most of his fear. He was hungry. They fed him scraps from their lunch. Even to set the crate down in the shade of a clump of bulrushes—where the closeness of the leaves and greenery made him feel more relaxed— seemed to serve as an act of compassion. They were beginning to discover that, in addition to their other talents, skunks can have charm.

Norman was studying this small pointed face through an open space in the crate, and he was intrigued by the sharp, needle-like teeth. He was almost tempted to offer a finger to give him a sniff.

"He might be cute, but you can't fool around with him," Gordon interrupted. "It's not like pettin' a cat, you know."

The skunk backed up and turned around in his box. The wind had blown the chaff out of his fur now, and the two white stripes, to the boys, were sheer beauty.

"What will we feed him at home?" came the next query.

This was a good question and, although it didn't get a response, it started some wheels turning in Punk Jordan's head—wheels that meshed in a rather unique and peculiar way. Punk, it seemed, got all of his original ideas from the association of ideas, and when someone mentioned food at the same time as he was sitting among the bulrushes, it somehow triggered memories of the lesson in Sunday School where Miss Keatch had been holding forth about poor Moses and his lowly beginnings. This was from the book of Deuteronomy. So, to Punk, the whole thing was intertwined—the bulrushes story is quaint, Deuteronomy is a mystery, the skunk is also a mystery, so why don't we call him Deuteronomy?

Even though they might have thought he was screwy, who could object? They needed a name, so why fight success? They named him Deuteronomy.

Leaving the bottom land, the prudent course seemed to be to avoid any wagons and buggies on the road. So they traversed the open fields, walking against the wind as much as possible so that the aroma might be carried in the opposite direction. The entourage stopped at intervals to rest. There was no rush. It seemed to be a well-thought-out plan that was working.

They came over the knoll behind some of the outer buildings of the village and were heading in the general direction of the cow barn, when their luck ran out. A team of unruly horses came up from the back driven by Young Hooley. He had bought the team of broncos a month previously and had never been able to get them to the blacksmith shop. As he passed close to the crate, the skunk moved quickly in his box, showing a flash of its white stripes. This spooked the bronco on the right side and caused him to rear up and leap sideways.

Young Hooley was a good horseman, but he couldn't cope with what happened. His rig lurched to the left and the back wheel of his Democrat caught the long board nailed across the top of the crate. The force of the lurching vehicle sent the whole party spinning in a circle, the flimsy chicken crate hit the ground and fell into pieces, while Deuteronomy gathered up all the dignity he could muster and headed across the vacant lot in the general direction of the main street.

It all happened so fast that nobody had time to think. But now they had to make a decision, and make it quickly. Should they follow the skunk and implicate themselves in any ruckus that might follow, or would it be better to hide the broken crate as soon as possible and play innocent of the whole affair? On impulse they tried to do both. Norman collected all the old pieces of wood and threw them onto a pile of debris behind the blacksmith shop, while the others followed on as interested onlookers.

Deuteronomy struck off across the vacant lot with his tail hoisted at full sail. He was the epitome of dignity and composure, drifting sideways, pausing and stomping his feet in warning when accosted by a yapping terrier pup who threatened to block his path. The terrier blustered in, then backed off as the first waft of stench entered his nostrils. At the watering trough in front of the livery barn, the ground was wet with over-spill. It seemed to offend the skunk's sense of decorum to have to walk through such slop, so he skirted the trough, lifting his feet high to avoid contamination.

By this time, three roustabouts from the livery stable were following at a respectable distance, so Deuteronomy moved closer to the buildings and followed the sidewalk. He passed the raised steps in front of the Gillespie store where three farm women went screaming inside, then stopped at the open door of Larry's Fattening Pen and Lunch Counter. He was about to enter but Larry happened to be mopping up a cup of spilled coffee at the time and headed him off with the mop.

News spread quickly from place to place, and people came running from all directions to see what was causing all the commotion. Kids, dogs, screaming ladies, and even ol' Oilcan from the machine shop came running with his squirt-gun. Gordon Didgey and Bobby Benton secretly hoped that Deuteronomy would take him on in a squirting duel, because they had had previous run-ins with Oilcan and they often suspected that he, too, had some concealed meanness glands.

Up to this point, their skunk friend had been able, in his own quiet way, to hold his own. True, he was not exactly a welcomed guest with everybody, and it was getting more difficult by the moment for him to cope with the mounting complications.

Train time was one-thirty in Quagmire, and the pace of traffic started to pick up. People were going to and from the station. Wagons that had been lined up at the elevators at noon hour now started to come off the ramps. Farm rigs were arriving in town to pick up groceries, and workers had now deserted the harvest fields and were drifting into town for the evening.

As Deuteronomy reached the end of the block, he was met by a flow of buggies and wagons turning onto the street. They cut off his passage and forced him right out into the moving mainstream. People formed up in clumps on the sidewalk to watch him manoeuvre, but his skills were not equal to the challenge. It was painful to watch.

A belligerent dog, seeing his advantage, got into the act and chased him into the front wheels of a dray wagon, and he spun in a circle while the back wheels ran clear over him and squashed him flat. It happened right across the street from the gospel tent, which had been set up by some revivalists from Moose Jaw that very morning, and Bobby heard one man say that it might ruin their evening service. The boys didn't care. The book of Deuteronomy had been closed, and his memory lingered on in a pall of stink.

Punk Jordan was mad. Gordon Didgey said that it didn't need to have happened. But practical Norman had an idea and didn't have time to stick around to explain. He headed home to the Benton basement and returned in a jiffy with a potato bag and a stick. He and his friends were about to play the role of undertakers and remove the remains for decent burial.

An earnest-looking man came out of the gospel tent to watch, while the traffic started to veer away from the smelly carcass. The boys moved in with open sack, forked the skunk in with their stick, took a good grip on the four corners of the bag and carried it off with dignity, while the onlookers laughed and applauded. No doubt the boys enjoyed being at the centre of the stage, but inwardly they thought that the clapping was a little out of place.

Once the procession passed off the street, traffic resumed and the entire incident could have been forgotten. The "fallen one" was carried back onto the prairie near the community hall and laid down on the grass. The boys then went into conference.

"He sure didn't have much chance, out there with that bunch of stubble jumpin' chariot drivers," Gordon Didgey remarked. "Maybe that's the way Dick Whittington lost his cat in London." Everybody moved up-wind from the body.

"If we could have kept him, Dad might have got the vet to take out his stink glands and we could have taken him all over the place like a pet," Norman wailed.

"But now he's dead and all we got is his fur and guts," Bobby added in utter disgust.

"There's more left than that," interjected Gordon. "There's still his stink glands, isn't there?"

And that thought opened up a whole new chapter of possibilities. Possibly there shouldn't be too much rush in getting the body buried? Possibly the people of Quagmire should not be allowed to forget Deuteronomy so quickly? Why should they not pay for some of their disregard?

"Why don't we find the stink glands and let them know that Deuteronomy cannot be easily forgotten?" Bobby added.

Gordon Didgey was quick to see what he was driving at. "All we have to do is git two chunks of tarpaper to put them between and we can have a stink-maker of our own," he added with enthusiasm.

"And it will be jist like Deuteronomy making his own protest," Bobby suggested.

Punk Jordan went home to find the tarpaper and Gordon and Bobby prepared for the operation. Gordon had a sharp knife in his pocket, so Bobby ended up holding one leg while he made the incision. Bobby was squatting on his haunches watching, because it was Norman who had read all the information about skunk anatomy in the Almanac.

Well, the Almanac was right again, because they located the two power-packed parcels right under the fat, low down on the belly. Norman removed them with care, being sure to get the nozzle part as well, without any great loss of the contained potion. When the vital parts were safely between sheets of tarpaper, they dug a hole with the Jordan shovel and buried the body beneath about ten scoops of prairie earth.

That night, when the village was alive with excitement, they decided to administer the first treatment.

Songs of joy and uplift were emanating from the revival tent on the vacant lot. The stores were full of people—some buying, others waiting their turn to get to the counters, and others just hanging around to visit. Rip Hogan's livery barn was full to capacity and sin may even have been taking place in the haymow.

There was a gentle breeze blowing from the north-west as the juvenile quartet moseyed back onto the prairie to find the stake that marked the spot. This was about the right distance to get complete coverage.

Gordon Didgey stepped forward, while the other three stood in a row with fingers to their noses. Then, as the full harvest moon shone down its blessing on the just and the unjust, he jumped up and down repeatedly upon the little black package.

The message floated out freely on the breeze and the whole downtown was quickly enveloped in the rapturous aroma.

Deuteronomy was triumphant. He was making his last stand!!

As one harvester from Ontario was moved to say, "This gumbo soil out here produces more than good wheat. If that don't let up soon, they can harvest it themselves."

6

STRAWSTACK LOGIC

WHEN winter came to the districts of southern Saskatchewan, it heralded a period of uncertainty that touched not only the many people who lived in outlying districts, but the groups of youngsters who trudged to the country schools. Yes, Quagmire now had a population of over eighty souls, but school districts had been established and some schools had been built even before Quagmire was on the map as a surveyed townsite. Political expediency, therefore, decreed that rather than build another school, students from the growing village could choose any of the four schools within five miles driving distance. The Weybridge school, which was three miles and a fraction, had the advantage that it was within walking distance, so it was usually the first choice.

At Weybridge, the windows were an ever-present distraction—two long rows down both walls, and cut just low enough to permit periods of untutored mind-drifting. The designers, no doubt, had come to the conclusion that there was nothing to see on the bald prairie, and therefore windows were no threat to scholastic development. They were wrong. Only yesterday a small herd of antelope had crossed the snow-covered stubble field, moving to the bluffs of the Comstock coulee. Miss Abercrombie had not seen them, but Gordon

Didgey and Bobby Benton had been watching them during the period when Grade Five was reviewing the travels of Radisson and Groseilliers.

The hours passed, and as the morning wore on, grey leaden clouds closed down to the horizon. Light feathery flakes floated and swirled in reversing formations at every skittish whim of the rising wind. Winter on the western plains could be a wondrous experience for all who ventured forth.

There were the regular hazards of travel, but it had its pleasures, too, for the young fry. Snow was dry and crunchy, and blew up in hard-packed drifts upon which they could run for miles in moccasin-clad feet. Moose-hide was considered to be the best. Thick felt insoles and two pairs of wool socks inside a pair of moose moccasins was almost a guarantee of warm feet. With this kind of gear, a healthy kid could run like a rabbit, and many of them actually did challenge the fleet-footed jack. At Weybridge it was not unusual to see a brigade of twenty kids or so form up at the woodshed, equip themselves with pieces of lath and proceed out into the surrounding fields in search of excitement. When the leader spotted one of the big western rabbits crouching behind a clump of tumbleweed or Russian thistle, they would all fan out in a wide arc to surround the crouching jack and gradually close ranks until he took fright and decided to make a run for the open spaces. Of course, no self respecting jack rabbit had any trouble escaping from an emotional crowd of screaming kids, but the exercise was exhilarating, and the teacher permitted such escapades because she thought it kept the boys more subdued in class.

On this particular day, they had all been out in the schoolyard making one of those large wheel-shaped patterns in the snow and were engaged in the time-honoured game of fox-and-geese during the recess period. Cheeks were flushed and mufflers matted with frozen breath when they came inside.

Chilly breezes were an everyday feature in mid-winter. Nobody thought anything of that. But, as Bill Benton had said, "Any time when the big dome closes down to the horizon, look for trouble." Outside, the sky had become a sombre frosty grey, and the wind rose, causing the eavestroughs to creak and a loose lightning-rod wire to slap against the building.

Miss Abercrombie had her hands full most of the time. She was a big lumpy woman from Ontario who had ventured out to the prairie frontier alone. Her stock in trade was correct spelling, neat handwriting and strict discipline. It was not hard to understand why she found the crude knife-carvings on the backs of the desk-lids so repugnant.

Teaching eight grades took some management, too. At the conclusion of Grade Three geography this day, young Willie Fender got up to go to the cloakroom, but while passing the squat floor-furnace at the back of the room, tossed a small metallic object onto the hot surface and marched nonchalantly on. He had made it at recess—a twenty-two calibre shell casing, from which he had removed the lead slug, replaced it with two match-heads and bent the end over tight with a pair of pliers. Right in the middle of Grade Five history, there was a detonation that sounded like one of Wolfe's cannons on the Plains of Abraham. Miss Abercrombie was nonplussed, but then, she was from Ontario and, to the prairie kids, that explained everything.

It also explained why she was conducting classes at two o'clock when the snow was starting to lash around the gables of the frame structure with increasing ferocity. Weybridge school had drawn its name from the notion that it might be somewhere mid-way between Weyburn and Lethbridge. That in itself might have been a cozy idea but, in a prairie blizzard, something more than fancy names is needed. The only protection the school had from the sweep of the elements was a few sprigs of caragana hedge surrounding the place and the page-wire gate at the road.

As Miss Abercrombie went to close the bookcase, a gust of wind caught the outer porch door and slammed it shut with such force that splinters of glass from its top panels showered over the floor. One sustained blast caused a tremor to convulse the walls. Then the shuddering ceased as the gale wheeled away to gather strength for a renewed assault. It was obviously time for clear and hard decisions.

"The weather does not seem to have cleared up," she announced. "In fact, it has become quite nasty out. If you children will take some work home with you, possibly we can adjourn for the day a few minutes early."

That seemed a pretty feeble concession, but nobody needed further elaboration. Mufflers, toques, pullover mitts, sheepskin coats and other warm garments were drawn from their pegs in an action-packed ten minutes of bundling. Since there were no telephones in the district at this time, there was no way to communicate to the parents at home. Everybody would soon be on their own in small groups.

The Chartrand boys ran to the barn to harness two shaggy Indian ponies. Alfie Millard, who drove the teacher to school, hitched Old Pelter to the cutter and arranged the buffalo robe around her feet. The remainder gathered in small clusters heading east, west and south according to destination.

The Quagmire group counted six—the three Bentons, Punk Jordan, Gordon Didgey and an Italian girl named Josie Natoli—all under eleven and all slightly apprehensive. It was three-and-a-half miles cross-country, but on a day like this they knew they must not leave the roads and the well-known landmarks. The hours of daylight in February are short. There would still be two hours to make home if they could keep moving.

At first it seemed fun to run on the hard banks with gusts of wind pushing them along. Some drifts had completely covered the fence posts. Little tongues of snow would speed swiftly across the surface; some places it accumulated in draws that were soft as pudding. The little flotilla was making good time until Josie, with her short legs, dropped into one of those long trenches at the mouth of a culvert. It might not have been any great scare to the boys, but by the time they had retrieved mitts, lunch pail, dignity and self assurance, another ten minutes of valuable time had been consumed. Josie's footwear wasn't any great shakes, either. Her mother didn't think that moccasins were very ladylike, and possibly they weren't—in Italy.

When the little party got back on course, it was not long before they were again engulfed in another blinding, swirling cloud of snow. This time snow was in their nostrils and eyes. It blew up sleeves and into the recesses in mufflers wound tightly around their necks. When the road became invisible they followed along the fence line, but the barbs on the wire played havoc with mitts and coat sleeves. Wind velocity was increasing; gusts came at closer intervals.

Punk Jordan was a stringbean sort of a kid. His dad didn't approve of the school aggregation calling him "Punk"; Jordan had been a soldier in the British army and said that "punk" was some sort of rotten bread. But rotten or not, Punk was a friend of the Benton lads and when it came to roughing it, he knew a thing or two. He was eleven, he played dibs like a professional, he had red hair and he was the same age as the oldest Benton, a fact that gave him status. So he and Norman took Josie in tow, while Gordon Didgey and his two younger cronies brought up the rear.

They had passed the old abandoned shack on the brow of the Bjerke hill, which was recognized as a two-mile landmark, when the wind changed. Now, facing into the storm, they felt the full fury in direct frontal attack. Drifts were blowing up great cornices. Snow crawled up the back of flanks. Fresh tracks filled in as fast as new ones could be made. At one time they lost sight of one another. Punk Jordan stopped to get his bearings and they all bunched together in a huddle with heads scrunched as deeply as possible into raised collars. Josie was whimpering, and Jamie had lost one mitt.

The time had come when clear thinking must prevail, and the Benton boys had been well instructed on possible actions to take in case of just such a contingency. Back of the derelict building across the fence, they knew there was a wooden granary, and beside every granary in those days there was bound to be a stack of wheatstraw left as dross after the harvest. These strawstacks dotted the prairie and were a haven for lost dogs, stray horses and all of the sundry who were in peril when blizzards swept the great open plains. The boys had been told many times that they could provide shelter for marooned school kids as well.

First, Norman drew the band into a compact group to explain strategy. Then, when the first lull came and visibility was temporarily restored, they left the road, passed through the fence and plunged through the soft snow lying in the stubble until all six had reached the door of the old shack. There, on the other side, was what they were looking for—the pile of straw—twenty towering feet of insulation. But it was covered with a thin crust of snow that had made it almost invisible in the storm.

Without stopping to appoint a foreman, or any of those other formalities of the adult world, the entire troop got down on their hunkers and took turns at digging straw, just as they had watched badgers hurling clouds of prairie dirt in spring in search of hibernating gophers. Even Josie did her stint as an excavator, if on a very limited scale.

Gordon Didgey had spotted a poplar pole leaning against the collapsed porch of the shack. He was off to get it.

"Keep diggin'," Punk shouted. "We've got to get this hole dug about fifteen feet into the stack and then make a room."

Late fall rains had packed the straw and made the digging difficult, but by the same token, this compacting was the best assurance against a cave-in. The tunnel progressed at an ever-diminishing speed because there was the problem of pushing out the straw that accumulated as the tunnel lengthened. A chain of bum-to-bum excavators moved the load along, but still the pace was telling. Finally they had fashioned a hollowed-out space large enough for them to stretch out full length.

The moment of accomplishment had come at last. The pole which Gordon had scrounged was thrust deep into the snowpile at the entrance, and Bobby volunteered his red muffler to be tied to it at full mast. When everybody was inside, the passageway was blocked with straw—just loose enough to allow for ventilation, but tight enough to keep out the snow and wind. The red muffler on the pole marked the spot where six animate bodies were entombed for the night.

Snuggled within the confines of their snow retreat there was some initial shuffling for position. Because she was Catholic, Josie's Sicilian upbringing prompted some misgivings about sleeping in a strawstack with five boys. Gordon eased her conscience somewhat by squeezing her in between Punk Jordan, who was also Catholic, and little Jamie. When all were satisfied, they huddled together in a compact ball as if they were Eskimos in an igloo.

Nobody had to stand up to turn off the lights. It was as dark as a cellar under the nearby deserted shack, and almost as spooky. There was the smell of musty straw and a great deadening silence, broken only by the fidgeting of shoulders and feet—quite a contrast to the wailing and howling of the storm outside.

Not a word was spoken for some moments. Then, "Holy Jupiter! Has anybody got anything left in their lunch pails?"

This rather urgent inquiry came from Norman, who was not one to stand on ceremony when it came to answering the pleadings of his stomach—and that was often. In response there was some squirming and twisting until the lunch pails were exhumed from the straw.

Quarters were so close in the dungeon that when lids were pried loose from the assortment of lard and honey pails, a unique mixture of smells permeated the cramped interior. The delicate aroma of peanut butter blended with sardines and salami. A few scraps were passed around—two leftover sandwiches, a cup of custard and a shriveled apple—all rejects from the noon-hour lunch. It wasn't enough, but it served as a pacifier.

"Anybody cold now?" asked Punk, after everybody had settled away again.

Nobody was cold, not even Josie, whose chattering teeth had come silent long enough to eat her share of a sandwich.

Somebody heaved a big sigh. More fidgeting. Gordon Didgey buttoned the flap on his collar, and little Jamie squirmed because Josie was still trying to stifle a recurring shudder. At this juncture, Punk, on the outside, turned to his left side, and everybody switched position in unison, ending up spoon fashion in close embrace. Shivering came to a quick stop as collective incubation pushed the common thermometer upward. Togetherness had its rewards.

"What if there are some mice in here?" little Jamie ventured.

"Don't be stupid," Gordon admonished. "They all go to California fer the winter, didn't ye know?" Gordon knew that questions like this were best squelched at once. Because he had always got one hundred percent in arithmetic, the other kids considered him a whiz.

But little Jamie had a talent for asking disturbing questions. He just changed the subject. "Sometimes I have to go to the toilet, you know," he murmured.

Punk decided that he should probably field this one. "If you want to wet the bed like a baby, wet your own side, you little squirt!"

Jamie was silent.

This conversation was followed by another resettling manoeuvre, where everybody pushed up an armful of straw for a pillow. As they settled back, Josie's wistful voice asked, "I wonder if all school teachers in Ontario are like Miss Abercrombie?"

Here was a chance to exhibit worldly knowledge, so Punk elevated the conversation to a loftier plain. "I know there are no Ontario teachers in Italy," he said, "but any we have out here are the same— *STUPID!*"

"No, they're not," interjected Norman, remembering his own Ontario connections. "When we went to school at Davyroyd, we had Mr. Spankey. He was from Ontario, and he was a good guy."

Brother Bobby kept out of the conversation. He wasn't particularly anxious to discuss the Davyroyd days, because there had really been no school there at all. In the absence of such a facility, Bill Benton, their father, had built a lean-to against the side of his homestead store and the neighbourhood chipped in so that they could hire Spankey from a list provided by the government. Being only three-and-a-half years old at the time, Bobby constituted somewhat of a problem. He couldn't be classified as a pupil, but they couldn't keep him from wandering around the classroom, either. So it seems that he spent almost three years in Grade One while he ran a shuttle service to the candy pails in order to keep on the good side of the older pupils. No wonder they all liked Spankey.

"He was a *MAN*," said Norman. "He taught us how to snare gophers, too."

Little Jamie, because of his sibling status, had been effectively barred from this conversation. He was too young to remember much about Davyroyd, but in spite of the professional tutoring offered by Mr. Spankey, he had learned from other kids how to snare gophers, so was off on another tack.

"Do they grow gophers in Italy, Josie?" he asked.

The Natali family had been in Canada for only two years. Josie's father worked for the C.P.R. as a section hand. He didn't speak very good English, but Josie had already gathered a fair command of the new language. The boys couldn't quite understand why she didn't brag as much as they did.

"In Italy, they don't have gophers, but they grow rabbits, and they make the meat into rabbit stew," she said. "I wonder what my mama is cooking for supper now?" she added with signs of a suppressed sob in her voice.

Little Jamie was quick to pick up the refrain. "Do you think they will come for us in this old strawstack?"

"Sure they will," answered Norman, but changed the subject in the very next second. "What is the earliest thing you can remember in your whole life?" he queried.

"Can you remember gittin' borned?" came a counter question from the prospective bed-wetter.

"No, but I can remember when you got borned," Norman shot back. "It was just before we moved to the new store at Quagmire, after the railway came through. Mother had to go to Moose Jaw in a buggy, and they brought you back for Easter."

Bobby said he could remember that. In fact, he started to remember a lot of things, some of the details somehow coming through a shroud of shadowy drowsiness. He remembered when the family had moved to the new townsite at Quagmire. It had been a warmer day; a day in the spring. There had been adventure in the air, but there was security, too. All at once Bobby could see himself again sitting next to his mother atop a pile of household effects that had been carefully loaded onto an old hayrack. His mother was sitting with him there on an old trunk and she was driving a harried team of horses.

There had been a cow in the picture somewhere. Yes, she was lurching along unwillingly at the end of a haltershank tied to the back of the rack. The team of horses was hauling this load across a long grade which had been pushed up in order that the wheeled vehicles could traverse the long stretch of bottomland known as the alkali flats. There were ditches on either side grown over with bulrushes, rank slough grasses and pools of stagnant water where ducks floated about and sandhill cranes came to feed.

At an eroded section on the grade, the cow lost her footing and slipped into a muckhole of soft mud. There was an anxious moment and Bill Benton, who was driving the lead team on a wagon up front, came running back to the rescue. After a session of encouragement, pushing and goading, old Bessie ended up back on the gravel road.

Bobby knew that he had been hallucinating, but when he broke through to consciousness once more, it was to hear the soft rippling snores all about him beautifully muted by the textured straw ceiling. He could feel a lock of the little Italian girl's hair flush against his cheek as she slumbered.

Sleep is an antidote for fatigue, but emotions can never be completely tranquilized. The excitement and uncertainty of the trek through the blizzard sent thoughts of peril skittering through his conscious mind, which again took refuge in the delirium of the interrupted dream.

But by this time the thread of continuity had been broken and other moments of concern from the past came drifting in from other unrelated experiences. And, no sooner had one episode disappeared into the shrouds of sleep, then another would come to take its place. The last one was climactic.

There he was on his hands and knees, crawling along under some piles of lumber at the Imperial yards, trying to catch a stray cat that somebody had turned loose in town for the winter. He followed it through a labyrinth of tunnels and under a pile of planks. It was a nice ginger-coloured cat, one that he felt his mother could not reject. So he continued to follow until suddenly he found himself firmly wedged between two upright supports under a pile of shiplap siding. There was nothing in there now but some crawling bugs and two black crickets that went skittering into a crack overhead. His hips were beginning to hurt. Bobby, in his delirium, was about to scream, when he heard his mother's voice.

"Are you boys in there? If you can hear us, yell!!"

It was her! And it was real!!!

"Over here, men! This looks like something familiar here, tied to the post. Sure, that's Bobby's red muffler!!" A horse snorted.

Suddenly every member in the strawstack sanctuary was awake. Within a second they were all jammed in the mouth of the passageway like a litter of coyote pups trying to get out of their den to greet the mother dragging home a piece of mutton.

As they dug from the inside, a windmill of flying hands clawed straw from the outside surface. Then came a burst of light and the chill air, heavy with morning frost. Toby, the Benton dog, pushed his nose through the loose sprigs of straw and slathered the first emerging face with a warm tongue.

The snow lay deep in the stubble, while a towering drift completely blocked sight of the granary, leaving a cornice running to the mouth of the cave. They stood back from the entrance and counted as each darling emerged. At the count of six, a noisy cheer went up. All present and accounted for.

Bill Benton, of course, was there, but so was Luigi Natoli. Jack Pomroy stood by with his team of dapple-greys hitched to a sleigh, while Toby barked and leaped about in crazy circles. Gordon Didgey's father was waiting with his earlaps full down, while Louisa Benton and

Mrs. Jordan clucked around, brushing the straw off toques and toting a jug of warm cocoa.

Well, a lot of hugging and crying went on there for awhile. There were emotional outpourings in two languages. Possibly old Jack Pomroy made the most sage remark, though. He just lit up his crooked-stemmed pipe, sent up a puff or two of smoke and said, "'Taint nothin'. Them kids ain't fools. It's jist strawstack logic, I guess."

7

CRAZY LIKE
THE CROW

*J*AMIE Benton stood looking up at the cardboard sign tacked on the wall at the blacksmith shop in Quagmire. The message read: "Bickmore's Gall Cure for Harness Burns and Heavy Chafing." What he couldn't understand was why the men should be interested in stopping chafing by harnesses but nobody cared what happened to the shaggy bronco the men were sitting on sprawled out on the sooty dirt floor while they tried to fit him out with a pair of iron shoes with cleats.

It took four men with ropes to hold down the spotted mustang while Jerry Culligan banged the flat nails into his hoofs and clinched them off in the claws of his hammer. The victim was an independent-looking cuss who had been running loose all winter. His cracked hoofs and a partially blind eye were evidence of a rough season, and he looked as though he had come to mistrust everything.

He sure didn't like being manhandled by this crowd, because he'd been there over an hour and they still had only three shoes installed. He was now lying almost upside down with ropes tied from his hind legs to the ceiling. One of the Jepson men was sitting on his head with a twitch on his upper lip, while Young Hooley was down on his knees biting his ear. The air was blue with profanity and heavy with the acrid smell of scorched hoofs.

"How'd you like someone burning patterns into your toenails?" Bobby protested.

"That's a crazy question," Gordon Didgey cut in. "They don't feel it when the nail goes through their hoof because Young Hooley is biting so hard on his ear he hasn't time to worry about his feet."

"I thought that's why they got a twitch on his lip," Norman interjected, still not satisfied.

"Maybe he's so mean they need both," Gordon added.

Suddenly the ropes were released and the horse gained his feet in two convulsive exertions. When Hooley pulled back on his halter, all could see that his hoofs were trim and the cleated steel shoes came down solid on the floor.

"Now, you kids all git the hell out of here before this mangy critter kicks yer brains out," shouted Jerry when he saw the audience he had attracted. He was grimy and wet with sweat, and the set of hot tongs in his hand looked quite convincing.

As they left the blacksmith shop that morning, it didn't seem to matter where they went, they seemed always to be running into horses. It was spring, and most farmers in the district were anxious to get working on the land. There was still some wheat from the last crop to be hauled to the elevators and a floundering team on a slippery road could be expensive and dangerous. Horses were important.

The boys wandered out to the corner and were about to return home when up the road, a two-wheeled cart approached. A heavy-set man wearing a battered felt hat was perched on the seat driving a bay mare of nondescript pedigree, but with a grander and more magnificent specimen of masculine horseflesh in tow. The sleek black stallion danced at the end of his haltershank just off the right wheel, his arched neck glistening while he toted a pair of knockers that looked like oversized pool balls carrying the sheen of black satin shoe polish.

"That must be Ebony Prince Charley," shouted Punk Jordan, pointing to the prancing steed. "The posters in Rip Hogan's livery stable have his picture an' everything hangin' in the office."

"Sure enough!" enthused Bobby, not wanting to be scooped on such an important piece of local happening. "I read it, too— 'Will be Standing at Stud at Five Dollars per Jump. March 31st and April 1st at Hogan Stables'." He had remembered the announcement to the last word.

Norman laughed mockingly. "He's not a jumping horse, ya nut. They have those in England for steeplechases."

"All right, ye'r so smart," Bobby quipped. "The poster also says, 'Repeat Service Guaranteed if Fertility Catch not Complete.' I suppose you think they jump steeples to improve their fertility, ya dumb cluck!"

"What's fertility?" asked little Jamie, wrinkling his freckled nose.

Gordon Didgey was laughing, and Bobby was just a little embarrassed. His own brother didn't know what a stud was for! The first reaction, of course, was that there should be a longer session with some details explained over in the wagon-box clubhouse. But a second consideration seemed to present the greatest challenge to their investigative natures. Possibly, with a little stealth and planning, they could see a first-hand demonstration of the Ebony Prince in action.

All day Saturday they kept a close watch on proceedings at the barn. There were the usual comings and goings. Teams of horses were allotted time for feeding in the various stalls, while their masters looked after such business as getting plough-shares sharpened and machine parts welded at the blacksmith shop. But other farmers brought along brood mares in singles and in pairs tied behind wagons. These, as Gordon Didgey pointed out, were to be "serviced" by the Ebony Prince. The puzzling thing, however, was that up to this time none of the boys even knew where he had been stabled.

It took some wily checking to locate the scene of activity and to discover a point of vantage from which proceedings could be observed. They thought of requisitioning the old pair of opera glasses in the Benton living-room. They knew, also, that if Rip Hogan or any of his gang at the barn caught them snooping, it would provide ammunition for jokes about the good people who went to church. So they determined that a quick reconnaissance was the first requisite.

Jamie and Bobby were to walk nonchalantly right past the open door of the barn, looking straight ahead as if they might be going down the street to the elevators. Meanwhile, Gordon and Norman would go in behind the buildings, climb over the manure pile and up the hay chute into the loft. By looking down through some of the apertures in the floor, it might be possible to pinpoint his whereabouts.

But this plan failed, and it wasn't until late in the afternoon that new evidence pointed to the fact that a completely different location was being used. By watching the pattern of traffic, and twice hearing an excited whinny, it was becoming obvious that a lean-to shed on the east side of the stable was occupied. It had been used to store empty barrels, barbed wire and bales of hay, but now all the clutter had been pushed back and there was plenty of space. During the fall election, this place had been used as a polling booth; ol' Rip Hogan had very appropriately left the sign tacked over the door.

The problem was to locate an observation point where their presence would go unnoticed, so the boys decided that the better part of valour was to wait until after dark. As soon as everything had gone silent, they piled old oil drums into position so that they could climb easily to the roof of the shed. Then, on the north slope of the roof, they lifted a couple of loose shingles, exposed a wide crack and then formed a canopy made from the same roofing, under which it would be possible to lie and watch proceedings. The stage was ready.

Next morning, the big subject of concern revolved around just when the first "jump" might be scheduled. Rafe Pinder was seen in the early hours, feeding up and scratching around the stalls with a fork. The watering trough had been filled to the brim and was down again to the normal mark. Rip Hogan had already whittled some Old Chum plug into his tobacco pouch for the day. The new men had gone into the shed with brushes and curry-combs. The opera glasses were ready for use.

In Quagmire, at this time of year, when the busy season was starting, everyone seemed to get a bit edgy. Winter had passed and there seemed to be more strangers moving about the country, possibly trying to get new work lined up for the season.

The young lads were up on the back of the building flattened out under their camouflage, when the first signal came that something was about to happen.

"Unfasten the rope on that black mare of Jack Pomroy's there in the box-stall and fetch 'er out." It was the voice of Rip Hogan calling to his flunky, Rafe Pinder, back in the barn.

Rafe came slouching out through the doorway with the mare's big Clydesdale feet almost tramping on top of his scruffy boots. There was horse slobber all down the front of his overalls. As he emerged into the daylight, a high-pitched whinny could be heard from the Ebony Prince next door. He was getting eager. Surely this was the moment.

If there ever was a bad time for destiny to give events another twist, it was now. Fate does insist on making its own decisions. And it would be difficult to guess who was the more disappointed with the turn of events—the sentinels on the roof or the thwarted stallion.

When Gaston Leblanc stumbled up to the front of the livery stable and fell down by the water trough, he looked like an escapee from some Alcatraz underground workings. Everybody recognized him by the old mackinaw cap that he wore both winter and summer, but nobody had ever seen him look this way before—a stubble of beard, matted black hair, sunken eyes and patched overalls black with coal dust. He regained his feet to get to the door of the stable but fell to the ground in front of Rafe Pinder and the black mare.

When Rip recognized the seriousness of the situation, he rushed to his office for a bottle of brandy. The others just scratched their heads. Gaston was no drifter. He lived in the ravine near St. Victor with his tall, slim half-breed wife and raised scrub cattle, mushrooms, potatoes and kids. In fall he often came to Quagmire to sell poplar poles because he said he didn't feel at home in bigger towns. But surely this must be the end of some tragic saga yet to be explained.

Rip got a few sips of brandy into him and a glimmer of life came back into his eyes. They thought he might soon be ready to talk.

"What the hell have you been doin', Frenchie? Tryin' to wrestle one of those Willow Bunch porcupines or something?" asked Rip, looking into his face.

With that, Gaston's eyes went shut and a tear rolled off his nose into the crop of dirty whiskers.

"Harriet," he kept saying. "Harriet, my wife, she's go loco, she's windigo! Looney, or what you call it."

In a moment they had him propped up and Mr. Parsons was coming with a cup of coffee and a bran muffin from Larry's lunch counter down the street.

"We'll just have to wait," Rip mumbled to some solicitous types who had started to crowd in. "You just can't push a man when he's exhausted."

In due time, strength started to return to his tortured frame, and with it a composure that was not exactly characteristic of Gaston. Possibly he was embarrassed at what he would have to relate. It certainly did not reflect honour and devotion on the part of his lifemate. But then he cast caution to the wind and let it all pour out.

"By Jeez, I was tole you, I'm lucky guy!" he said, shaking his head. "Firs' she's got excite an' try bus' up my nose. Den she grab de beeg knife an try to cut my t'roat. W'at I tol' you—dat's de troot—she's chase me for two t'ree day."

People in Quagmire had had dealings with Frenchie and his string-bean wife, but there was little discord and nothing more than was considered normal. At their establishment back in the hills, the Leblanc household had come through good times and bad, raised what cattle they could find pasture for, planted an annual crop of potatoes and corn, grew mushrooms in summer and set traps for muskrats and coyotes in the water. Harriet carried a generous portion of the Sioux blood that remained in the Willow Bunch district after Sitting Bull had been taken back to the Dakotas. She was just the strong and resourceful woman that Gaston needed. She knew the country to the last hummock, picked Saskatoons in the ravines, bathed in the creeks and cooked wholesome food for their family. Gaston kept on good terms with the parish priest, played his violin for recreation and kept the babies coming. As he said to Bill Benton one day in the store, "We fit togadder like we was spliced like dat."

Obviously everything had changed, and Gaston was now on the run.

"For long tam I notice she's got look in her eyes like she's lost," he continued. "Maybe she's got sickness wit' dat change-of-life beezness. Doc La Fleur talk to me about dat ting an' I guess I not listen, me."

Whatever malady had come to possess her, Harriet had gone off the deep end. One morning she had come at him brandishing a butcher knife and Gaston was so frightened that he took to the hills with Harriet in hot pursuit. If she had given him time to put some distance between them, Gaston explained, he might have sought help to get her subdued. But Harriet was too fast a runner for that. She followed him back into the coulee brandishing the lethal blade over her head and uttering war whoops he had never heard before.

At first it seemed good sense to be running away from the house. In this frame of mind the children might not be safe in her presence, and he did not want to be struck down before their eyes. On the other hand, he knew that on a long sprint of endurance, he could not hope to win. There was only one hope left—the old abandoned coal-mine shaft in the side of Lalonde Coulee.

Blood was surging fast through every vein in his body as he put on the final burst of speed that brought him to the dark deserted entrance of the mine. It looked like a collapsed navel with bits of rubbish and scrap lumber scattered about the entrance. There was an estimated five minutes remaining in which to drag some of the debris into the mine and then barricade the entrance from the back with discarded mine props, rocks and other assorted clutter.

Here at the open door of the livery stable, the gathering crowd was still growing. Some lingered through curiosity. Others showed a genuine human concern.

For the boys, up on the back slope of the roof, the sudden turn of events had come as a complete surprise. The black mare had been turned around and led back to her stall, so they decided to leave their observation post and mingle with the gathering on the street level.

Gaston was no stranger to the Benton lads. They had unpacked and counted eggs that he occasionally sold at the Benton store. As they made a circuitous route around the back of the barn to avoid appearing conspicuous, they could see that Bill Benton himself was now joining the crowd. Being a notary public in the community, they thought, his help would possibly be necessary.

"In my 'ol life," Gaston was explaining, "dat was de wors' tam I yet be see. At night I don' sleep cause I hear her footprints, an' by Jeez, at morning I tink she still be dere. She's come col' in dat place like you never believe."

"Well, Bill, what do you think we should do?" Rip Hogan was actually talking to Bill Benton, and with a hand firmly planted on his shoulder.

To the disheveled Frenchman, there was only one answer. "Mes chers amis," he interjected, "why do you t'ink I ron ten mile to Quagmire? For my life, I don' care me, but I am skare for my keed! You can telephone Assiniboia? You mus' git police!"

Obviously Gaston had been thinking. There were no telephones in St. Victor, but from Quagmire it would be possible to put a long-distance call through to Assiniboia over the community system that had just been installed, and the police might be able to get out with a speeder on the C.P.R. tracks. From Quagmire, Rip Hogan or some of the boys could drive them to the Leblanc homestead.

Bill Benton had a few words with Gaston and got him to his feet. They started for the store and, in order that they should know all the details when the call went through, Rip and his understudy, Young Hooley, were invited to come along as well. Four boys in bare feet brought up the rear.

As the party entered the front door, the tag-alongs slipped in and disappeared quickly behind a pile of cartons in the stockroom, where most of the conversation could be heard.

The men were gathered around the varnished wooden box on the wall, and the small handle was grinding out a raspy dingle. "You talk to dem police guy, Bill," Gaston was suggesting. "I get all excite me w'en I talk on dat gadget."

The call went through in an atmosphere of tension. There was the usual series of clicking noises that could be heard even in the stockroom, and finally the connection was made; a few preliminary introductions and then the authoritative voice of an officer at the other end.

Benton was explaining how a Mr. Leblanc had arrived in Quagmire with a harrowing story about an escape from a coal-mine hideout. Then he spelled out the letters of the first name H-A-R-R-I-E-T, and mentioned the place of residence as St. Victor.

"Is that true?" Benton asked again, with incredulity hanging in his words. "But how did she ever get that far?"

When Gaston caught these snatches of information, his tongue raced ahead. "Maybe she's go to her seester in Willow Bunch? Maybe she's go talk to de pries'? Maybe she's drink too much cognac?"

Well, it was none of these possibilities.

When Benton hung up the phone, it was to inform everyone that Harriet had walked the fifteen miles to Assiniboia in search of her lost man. She was almost incoherent in her speech and had been found wandering the streets in her gingham dress, a tattered straw hat on her head and with one bloomer leg hanging below her knee. The knife had long since been discarded and she was now in a mood of deep remorse.

Louisa Benton, by this time, had come into the store through a side entrance and had caught vital parts of the conversation. She suggested that if they would all care to move into the living-room of their adjoining home, there was better seating accommodation and they could continue the discussion while she fixed some coffee.

A few minutes elapsed before they had all straggled through to the living quarters. Gaston, his mind churning thoughts like the coffee mill in the kitchen, suggested that they should lose no time. They should go directly to Assiniboia and pick her up at once.

"Maybe she bus' up my nose. I don' care me. She is still my woman," he reasoned.

But Bill Benton knew he had a work of diplomacy to accomplish, and he was casting about for the smoothest approach he could find. "There is no use to complicate the situation further just now," he suggested. "Your good wife, Harriet, has been put in the care of some of Assiniboia's best doctors and everything is being done to make her comfortable."

"But she mus' come home to look after little Giselle, our baby," Gaston whimpered.

"The town doctors say she will have to go to Weyburn for treatment, and the mere fact that she sees you, Gaston, might throw her right back into a violent mood again. They say there is a narrow margin between love and hate, and that is one of her problems." Benton was no psychiatrist, but he was making it as convincing as he knew how.

But Gaston bowed his head and tears ran down his face. "Dat's no place to put de woman," he protested. "Dat bug house, she's worse dan de jail!"

Louisa Benton passed him a cup of hot coffee with a reassuring smile. "Last year a friend of mine, Mrs. Pembleton, had to go there with 'that sickness'," she said, "and today she is back with her fine family in Readlyn."

Well, there had been events of tragedy in the young life of the Quagmire community and there would be more, but the sweeping prairie with its electric storms and chinook winds was the greatest leveler of them all. There, in the inner sanctum of the Benton household, sat a man whose hopes of happiness had seemingly been shattered and there, as his angels of mercy, sat the infamous Rip Hogan and Young Hooley with manure on their boots, drinking coffee out of Louisa's good bone china brought from Ontario for special guests.

After a period of time, when the conversation had almost died, Rip Hogan rose to his feet, took Gaston by the arm and in a low voice said, "Come on, Frenchie. It's gettin' late. We'll hitch up the team of bays in the back stall there and be in St. Victor in less time than it takes to argue about it. We'll gather up yer kids, make a visit to the priest, and see what decision seems to be the best for everybody."

That was one suggestion that Gaston could fall in with at once, so they went out the door together.

"Thanks for the coffee, Mrs. Benton," said Rip in departing. "Tell yer kids they kin play in the haymow any time they want, jist so's they don't bring matches."

As the team of bays drove off up the road with Rip Hogan and his passenger riding along in deep conversation, Bobby and Norman had a few words with their mother about the whole Leblanc episode. It was one thing to figure out just how old Rip had made it to their living-room with his foggy shoes, but what was wrong with Harriet? Louisa Benton did her best, but some gaps were bound to remain in the details.

The boys left the store and crossed the road toward the blacksmith shop. On the way, however, they noticed one activity that they could understand—a horse-drawn cart was going up the road with a fine ebony black stallion jogging along at the rear wheel, and the sun glistened off his curried flanks.

"Damned fate," Jamie mumbled. "Now we got to wait 'til next trip, whenever that will be."

Precisely a year after that day, early in the forenoon, Gaston Leblanc rode into Quagmire from St. Victor. He proceeded to buy an unusually large bag of groceries at the Benton store.

But this time he came for something more than just the groceries. When the 12:45 passenger train arrived from Weyburn, Harriet stepped off with a smile and open arms.

Like Gaston once said on another occasion and under completely different circumstances, "Life, she's crazee like de crow—dey fly one in bunches and t'ree all alone."

And, incidentally, there were a lot of black colts born in the Quagmire district that spring, too.

8

COYOTES
ARE PEOPLE

*I*N the spring of 1918, creeks in the coulees near Quagmire were swollen to overflowing, and the great alkali flat at the bottom of Johnson Lake was a continuous sheet of slush and rubber-ice. Spring had come late. The heaps of snow that had accumulated in February remained through March, and it was the middle of April before glimpses of green grass showed through the mantle of dirty snow on the slopes of the hills.

As days lengthened out and the great melt continued, residents of the village gathered around in the evenings just to listen to the arrival of spring. Endless flocks of geese, with their wild and haunting continuous honking, passed over like streams of confetti strung out in the heavens. Creeks in the coulees filled to the brim, spilled over their banks and flooded low-lying meadows. In the still of the evening, the sound of rushing waters was ominous; bridges and earthen dams that had been constructed to hold back the runoff for cattle were now holding back their greatest load. Occasionally a rumbling roar meant that someone's dam had washed out in a swirl of mud and soggy gravel.

At the country school, studies had become tedious. Learning how to determine the amount of wallpaper required to cover a hypothetical room had lost all of its challenge. The Quagmire kids were all waiting for the twenty-fourth of May, Queen Victoria's birthday. When the big day rolled around, it was only routine that the Benton exploratory party was ready for another of those sorties that had no declared purpose, but was dedicated to snoop out and investigate any and all phenomena of intrinsic interest.

Shortly after breakfast, the four pathfinders headed back into the ravines behind the Quagmire community hall—Norman, Bobby, Jamie and their boon companion Gordon Didgey—fully equipped with such essentials as string, jack-knives, cookies, gum and chocolate bars. The earth was strewn with blotches of purple crocus-bloom and buttercups with petals so glossy that they seemed to have been licked clean. This was the sort of day they would wander farther afield—past the abandoned tarpaper shack, through the first ravine and into the stony rolling country in the range of hills beyond. This was the badland, considered fit only for badgers and grazing sheep. The gopher population was even more prolific here, and already the young were scampering around in the warm sun, always tempted to stray too far from the freshly dug mounds.

A situation like this, of course, could hardly be overlooked by small boys, so it should not be unexpected that a new game was devised. By standing quietly until a batch of young gophers had wandered a careless distance from their hole, then making a lightning rush and sitting over the mouth of the main entrance, it was possible to sit and watch the young scurrying and scrambling to get in somewhere, even though it sometimes meant running up a pantleg or into a fold in an open shirt. Jamie and Bobby thought it was thrilling, but Norman said they were "juvenile."

Up ahead, the shoulder of the hill dropped off dramatically, revealing the gouged-out shape of an abandoned gravel pit. Their approach to the spot was so sudden that a small, brownish-grey animal was seen to make a headlong dash for a concealed den hidden by the hanging overburden of grassy topsoil. The small creature disappeared completely.

"What do you suppose that was?" Gordon queried, as he arrived breathlessly at the edge of the overhang.

"Badgers don't dig under ledges," Norman observed with feigned knowledge, "so we can forget badgers."

Jamie, who had not been a participant in the capturing of a live skunk on a former occasion, warned that an attack by fumes was a distant possibility.

"We haven't got any shovel here, so let's jist make a guess where the end of the den might be, an' dig straight down with our hands,'' Norman suggested.

The others warmed to the idea and were already snooping around in the grass on the top of the ledge. "Any beast would git pretty tired diggin' by the time he got this far," said Gordon, kicking the turf loose about ten feet back from the edge.

It was just a wild guess, but he couldn't have located the right spot better with complicated sounding equipment and a steel measuring tape. They scratched away sod and some gravel, then lifted a piece of flat shale rock free from its socket. As the flat stone came up, loose morsels of sand and tufts of grass tumbled back into the cavity. The shafts of warm spring sunlight revealed six furry, cringing coyote pups huddled together.

"Holy kriminently!!" Gordon burst with excitement. "Jist look at that!"

Litters of coyotes had been dug from dens in the district before. The boys had previously seen coyote pups sunning themselves around the mouth of a den on the south slope of a hill. But here was a whole conglomeration of heads, feet and tails that could be inspected at close range.

"They all got fat bellies, but skinny ribs," Jamie reported, with his head down the hole almost to his shoulders.

Then it was Bobby's turn. "They all got bugs stickin' out all over in their fur," he declared. "Bugs that's got their heads buried under the skin and big bums stickin' out like seeds on those weeds Ma calls Shepherd's Purse."

Norman Didgey guffawed. "The stupid ass don't know they're sheep ticks."

"You know, I think they're sheep ticks," Bobby announced, coming up for air. "That ol' Flummerfeldt guy who raises sheep back here—I betcha they're from his flock. They have their eyes open," he continued, "so they must be at least six days old."

Closer examination established that the coyotes were infested, all right. A small piece of sheep carcass with the wool still attached confirmed the theory.

"They'll all die if we leave them here," said Jamie.

"Even if they don't die," Gordon interjected, "they'll jist keep eatin' up ol' Flummerfeldt's sheep." A very convincing statement.

And Norman went on to tell about an Indian fellow he had met at Wood Mountain who kept a coyote right in his house.

When everything was taken into consideration, there seemed only one decent, logical thing to do—rescue the pups from a miserable end, remove them from such a lousy environment and take them home to Quagmire immediately. The mother was away, doubtless to kill more sheep, and she'd be glad if someone else could give them a better way of life.

Gordon Didgey stood guard at the den while Norman and his young brother went to the old shack in search of a box. In due course they returned carrying a cardboard carton with the faded outline of a ketchup bottle still visible on its side. That was just the ticket—a thin layer of grass in the bottom, then the contents of the hole transferred and the lid carefully closed.

At approximately one hour from that moment, the lid was again opened and the six coyote pups dumped out onto the carpet in the living-room at the Benton home.

Louisa Benton was dumbfounded. "What, in the name of Jupiter, have you kids got yourselves into now?" she exploded.

"Orphan coyotes," said little Jamie, his freckled face just aglow. "They ain't happy 'cause the sheep ticks are suckin' their blood. We saved them," he elaborated with pride.

Mrs. Benton was a woman who could be firm when it came to enforcing such rules as washing feet and carrying in wood, but in matters of compassion, her sternness faltered badly. Jamie knew the soft spots and so did the others. Before realizing what was happening, she was completely engaged in the work of reclamation.

De-ticking was a matter of employing a technique that she had already mastered. The Saskatchewan ticks, she said, "respond to the same treatment as they do in Ontario," and she demonstrated how the tip of a hot needle, applied to the rear end of a tick, or to the point where it has attached itself, will induce it to cease sucking and let go. For the next hour, the four humans kept steadily engaged at lifting these ugly parasites off the hosts and dropping them in a cup. From there, they were conveyed to the hot coals in the kitchen range and thence to oblivion. The tick problem had been conquered.

Furthermore, and before she realized her deepening involvement, Louisa Benton became an instructor in the feeding and care of coyote pups as well. She resurrected an eye-dropper from a cluttered drawer, held each little beast upside down in the palm of her hand and just kept the flow of warm milk dripping into their greedy little gullets until their appetites were satiated. At this point they snuggled together in drowsy contentment.

By that afternoon, and before father Benton had a chance to register disapproval, the task of preparing quarters for the brood was well advanced. A wooden framework, constructed mostly from wooden packing boxes, was covered with chicken wire, and at one end the passage was narrowed to simulate a den. An old discarded floor-cover provided the necessary darkness, and the whole ramshackle collection was located at the rear of the Benton store, protected from the wind and out of sight of people and dogs. The Quagmire Coyote Nursery had been established.

Spring days grew longer and warmer as the season advanced. Every day the pups grew bigger and more playful. Rough and tumble encounters became routine behind the wire enclosure. They were fun to watch, but feeding time could best be described as an exercise in bad manners. At times Louisa Benton wondered whether the example might not influence behaviour at her own table.

By the end of June the pups would eat anything, but for sheer chomping ecstasy nothing could replace raw meat. On one occasion, a live gopher ran through the mesh wire thinking it was going to find refuge from a pursuing dog. Before anyone could pronounce the "go" in gopher it was gone—ripped asunder by a yapping, yanking den of demons in a display of savagery that would cause a stone statue to shudder.

Another aspect of the wolf temperament became apparent with the passing of daylight. The setting of the sun seemed always to be accompanied by a change of mood. One night Norman stood near the pen casually playing a tune on his mouth organ and was surprised indeed when the first few mournful strains of "Annie Laurie" were accompanied by a chorus of high-pitched yapping from the soprano section, punctuated by a weird staccato and ending in a sustained, deep-throated howl. The next verse, of course, brought on such a chorus of unrestrained ebullience that it attracted an audience from the pool room and the livery barn, while the "owners" basked in notoriety.

Feeding the menagerie now consumed a lot of effort. The Benton kids ranged far afield for mice, rabbits, gophers, and once even considered dispatching a stray dog that continued to give trouble around the pens. However, when Norman came down one morning, it was to find that some of their problems had already been solved. Excavation proceedings were well advanced. Four pups had disappeared and a fifth was standing outside the wire cage sniffing noses with his friend on the inside. For some unexplained reason, he was either reluctant to go or too stupid to find the escape hatch. Norman made a rush to secure the hole, while Bobby took off after the only other fugitive in sight.

The little wolf led him a rigorous chase—back across the prairie as fast as the coyote could drive those rangy legs, looking back over his shoulder at intervals to make sure that the pursuit was still in progress. As he slipped over the brow of the hill he found better footing on a rabbit path, and the straw-grey ball of fur disappeared from view.

For a moment Bobby searched the spot. A few minutes ticked away and he was about to give up when the outline of a pair of ears was spotted, flattened against the coyote's back and partially concealed in the deep grass. Bobby made a lunge for him, but the reaction came as a complete surprise. In a frontal flying attack, the little fiend flew savagely at Bobby's pantlegs, scratching and biting as though it was his final fling. Although surprised, Bobby reacted in kind, stunning the animal with a well-placed kick. In this condition Bobby was able to regain control, lashing the wolf's feet together with a handkerchief—not a bad manoeuvre for a kid in bare feet.

When Bobby returned his captive to the pen, it was to find the "loyalist" sitting passively on little Jamie's knee, looking off into space and whimpering. Somehow a special relationship had taken root between the smallest Benton and the temporary orphan. During this period of loneliness, Jamie had adopted him as his own and even given him a name. He liked the colour of the long fur on his flanks, so he called him Rusty.

Yes, when the sun went down that July evening, only two members of the pack remained—one by choice and the other with bruised ribs and bitter feelings. The rest of the escapees went back to where all coyotes go when they are in search of a full life of prairie coyotehood—to the coulees.

That summer there were other big changes in store for the Benton lads. Norman had just passed out of Grade Eight. There was no high school in Quagmire, and rumour had it that Bill Benton was looking around to buy a small house in the nearby town of Burdock, so that the boys could all go there to attend high school.

At first the idea was very disturbing. Bob was in Grade Seven and Jamie in Grade Six. So why was it necessary to leave the creeks and the coulees just to attend a town school? And besides, who was going to look after the coyotes?

But, as the first of September rolled around, it was obvious that the inevitable change was going to take place. One Sunday at dinner, Bill Benton explained that he had bought a small, stucco two-room shack with a shed at the back of the lot. The three boys would be going there to live during the week and would be able to return to Quagmire on weekends when the weather permitted. He said that it was a small building, but in time a closed-in verandah could be added and, if the boys would dig a basement under the back end, he would have a carpenter build a kitchen over it to adjoin the house.

When he inquired whether or not there were any comments about the place, there were two questions—"Who is going to do the cooking?" and "Where do we keep the coyotes?"

As the day of the scheduled move came closer, plans evolved in more detail. Mrs. Benton would be staying with the boys for the first month, at least, to make sure that methods of preparing meals and general housekeeping habits were established. A load of oatsheaves and hay would be delivered to the shed in order to feed a cow—possibly next year. The bulk of the groceries would come up from the store in Quagmire each weekend with the returning students. One person would likely have to remain at the shack some weekends in order to keep it up.

But what about the coyotes?

"If Rusty isn't going, I'm not, either," Jamie announced with the suggestion of a blubber trembling on his lips.

But Bill Benton was taking the important things first. "You fellows will have to look after your mother the same as she looks after you. There will be some spending money, but you will have to learn to find ways to make a little extra for yourselves. Possibly you can earn enough to pay for books and other incidentals, but if there is any sports equipment you have to buy, we'll get that for you from the wholesale catalogues at the store here. So you will have the best baseball gloves and bats in your class."

That sounded good, but still it did not answer the question about the coyotes. Jamie was just gearing up to cut in again when father Benton headed him off.

"That's all been looked after, too, Jamie," he added with a hand on the shoulder. We won't be sending the cow up this season so, in the meantime, why not keep your coyotes tied up in the shed?"

That seemed to settle everything. Moving day came and the big shift was made. There were things forgotten and dislocations in many other departments, but the two gangly-legged coyote pups found themselves appropriately fitted with leather collars and able to run at the end of a length of chain that was anchored beneath a discarded old washing machine—their new den.

It was not difficult to become acquainted in Burdock. With coyotes for pets, the Bentons enjoyed instant popularity. Not every town kid could have wild animals for pets.

The first month could be described as a settling-in period. The boys made acquaintances with new classmates at school and the coyotes became more familiar with the new surroundings. Scraps from the table and bones from a downtown butcher shop provided a pretty healthy diet for the young demons and, as the season advanced, their grey-brown fur became more deep and silky. Rusty, who was a male, became tamer. His sister, Mabel, remained more withdrawn.

Toward the end of the month, when everything seemed to be running smoothly, coyote-neighbour relations took a turn for the worse. Early one morning, the Benton household was aroused by frantic knocking on the back door. Mrs. Benton, dressed in her night attire, answered the call. From their beds, the boys could hear her voice. "Just a moment, I'll call the owner."

There was a confused moment. Just who was the owner? Bobby, because of his middle position, was forced into the role of responsibility. He took his stance at the door, to be faced by a wild-eyed matron whom he recognized as Mrs. Kuplinski from across the street. In her hand she held the mangled body of a white Wyandotte hen, while she hurled curses in three different languages, ending in English.

"You stupid keed," she concluded. "You try to make zoo, and you only make beeg trouble. Your coyote keel my cheeken, so I keel your coyote an I don't geev a damn!!"

With these words she made an abrupt withdrawal, and all diplomatic relations were suspended forthwith. The boys didn't even go to reclaim the body, for fear of getting the same neck-yoke broken over their own heads.

It was a morning of tragedy, but the misfortune was somewhat tempered by the fact that it was Rusty who had been spared to become sole heir to all the choice bones that had been buried from time to time in the yard. Mother Benton called her own pups together and explained that people in big places like Burdock sometimes did not take kindly to newcomers who had pets that created odours and got loose to cause havoc, so Rusty's chain was double checked and well anchored. They concluded that it might be easier to handle one coyote on a twelve-foot chain than two coyotes getting tangled on shorter lengths and exciting each other. The twelve-foot chain seemed ideal for a twenty-five foot lot, they reasoned, because the neighbour to the immediate left had chickens, too. Jamie suggested that they should think of Rusty as their watchdog.

In this setting, the coyote seemed quite content. Rusty just sat in the doorway of the shed watching the fat hens pecking aimlessly about wherever the scattered grain might led them. Within the radius of the chain, there was a thin sprinkling of oat kernels from the pile of sheaves that were stored inside. But they were Benton kernels. On occasion, the odd hen would come leisurely pecking her way through a hole in the fence and, while Louisa Benton fidgeted with fear, Rusty just sat there looking inscrutable.

Day after day he allowed hens to wander into his domain without the least show of interest. He seemed always to be deeply absorbed in some complicated problem in analytical geometry. Then one day, like a comet, a silver streak shot through the air, two quick shifts of direction, a lash of his bushy tail, and Rusty was up to his ears in feathers. The hens in the adjoining yard went screeching to their shed in disarray, a screen door flew open and shut, and there was general confusion. But Rusty had solved his mathematics exercise, and he had done it legally.

Proudly, the quarry was hauled off to his den. He was munching bones and ripping sinews when Louisa made it to the door of the shed with Jamie and Bob close at her heels. Then and there, she decided to teach him a lesson. She was whacking him good with a flat board, when Norman reminded her that she was beating a wolf.

"He's not a dog, you know, he's a coyote," shouted little Jamie. "You don't whip coyotes, you train them. It says it in the book!"

Jamie was proven right. Mrs. Benton patched up the affair with the neighbours, the fence was fixed over so that further chicken killings would be avoided, but Rusty never forgave nor forgot. He never fraternized with her again.

Occasionally neighbourhood dogs would wander into the yard in a mood for reciprocal nonsense. Sometimes a clumsy elated pup would make the mistake of undue familiarity. Rusty would cavort with them until he was bored with the visit, then administer a savage nip to send them howling. A moment later he could be seen sitting in the doorway of his shed again looking inscrutable.

With the first fall of snow, the coyote was almost full grown. His fur was luxuriously soft and deep, and his ears stood up sharp when unusual noises attracted his attention. He was a beautiful specimen.

The Benton boys were still going home to Quagmire on week-ends, but days were getting shorter now, so they went on Saturday mornings. There was always a fuss at the store when they arrived. Bill

Benton was glad to get his family home but usually had to wait until evening to visit because customers had to be served. The lads usually seized this opportunity to get off to their old haunts in the ravines and coulees.

This particular trip was more special, because they were bringing back one of the native sons—Rusty the Coyote, sired in the hills, born in a gravel pit and saved from a scourge of coyote-eating sheep ticks.

The boys took off over the hills as though they knew every inch of the terrain. A soft mantle of snow lay over everything. The sun was bright in a pale-blue sky. It was one of those days in early winter when the snow was antiseptic white and the air was bright and exhilarating. Summer birds had disappeared, and there was almost a dead silence in the hills. Walking through the crunchy snow created sufficient sound to flush up a crouching grouse and send it splitting the air with whirring wings. Rusty was in his element.

Back in the coulee near the old tarpaper shack, they paused just to watch him root his nose under the snow to pick up different scents.

"What do you think would happen if we took off his collar?" Norman ventured after some deliberation.

"He'll git chasin' a rabbit or something an' that's the last we'll see of him," Bob suggested.

But, with little Jamie, again it was a matter of blind trust. "He's our friend," he insisted. "He can't stay away, even if he wants to."

So Norman reached down and unbuckled the collar. Rusty didn't fuss. He just looked around as though he was in deep thought. Then he crouched down on his paws in the loose snow and sprang forward with a flash of his furry tail. Head down, and tail looped in a silly arch, he raced in wide circles, going far afield as if to tease, then coming in close at breakneck speed to finish the circuit with a headlong plunge into a bank of fleecy new-fallen snow. In a flash he emerged looking like a dazed and ludicrous ghost, fully ready to stage a repeat performance at the drop of the hat.

It was an exciting exhibition, but there was an element of apprehension about it all. Would it be really possible to get him back on the chain?

Bob decided to test the situation, so he started to blow a whistle through his upturned thumbs. It was a familiar sound and caused Rusty's ears to perk up, but he continued in another smaller circle. Norman had a try, but the coyote shied off at the sight of the collar. Then Jamie went out in the field, lay down in the snow and started to loll and whimper. Rusty manoeuvred around, sniffed at his mitts and stood still while the collar went back around his neck.

106

From that moment forward, there was little question of who was Rusty's "owner."

With the approach of spring, the call of the coulees again became an impelling force. From every ravine, the sound of rushing water was music in the still of the prairie night. The smell of freshly plowed fields, of slough grass, of crocus blooms and the sight of fresh badger mounds was enough in itself. But when the flights of mallard ducks and the long files of honking Canada geese started their migratory journey, Rusty looked so dejected sitting in his doorway that they decided to take him again to the Quagmire district for a nostalgic weekend.

School was scheduled to recess again for the Victoria Day holiday. This was the coyote's anniversary of inception into the civilized world. The holiday would fall on the Monday, so they decided to return to Quagmire on Friday night after school in order to gain the longest possible respite from books and teachers.

Saturday morning they started down the railway tracks toward the long wooden trestle near the Woothey farm. Out on the green slope on the bank of the rampaging creek seemed a good place to slip the collar off Rusty's neck and let him run again. It all seemed so traditional now.

As usual, he took off down the bank of the stream, stopped for a drink, sniffed at some gopher excavations, made a wide arc back over the hill and disappeared down the next ravine. The boys busied themselves trying to dam up the water with stones and mud so that later in the season there might be enough held back for a place to swim. They were deeply involved, so the time went fast. When Rusty had not returned in an hour, the feeling of concern changed to alarm. If he was going to leave, surely he wouldn't do it that way.

Norman walked to the top of the hill and the other two followed him down into the steep, eroded gulch below.

This was the place where they had hauled the dead horses after the big accident on the rail right-of-way three years earlier. There was another carcass there now—a roan mare with sprigs of green grass pushing up through wisps of tail hair strewn over the ground.

But there was something else there as well. A contorted grey-brown shape, a head with tongue extended and glassy eyes.

Strychnine kills wolves, but this day it also killed a friend.

9

HIGHER EDUCATION

*F*OR the three Benton boys, that first year at Burdock High was a clinker. At home in Quagmire, the fact that they had a pet coyote guaranteed a certain amount of popularity, but in Burdock things were different. There was the big brick school building with electric lights and running water to get accustomed to. There was the social necessity to change from an almost aboriginal attachment to the coulee country to a more organized state of human relationships. When he registered for school the first day, Bob explained to his mother that it was like entering a big palace full of books and polished people, while he stood dressed in fleece-lined underwear waiting for somebody to laugh.

There was not only the problem of wearing different clothes. For the first time, they had to contend with girls—more gregarious girls.

At Quagmire they had learned to wrestle by the Marquis of Queensbury rules, and they thought that was the general practice. In Burdock, it seemed that to win a match was to invite a fight, not only with the elected adversary, but with all of his relatives. On one occasion, Bob floored a Burdock tough in the school gymnasium, then the next older brother, and finally was surprised to find an older one lying in wait for him when school was dismissed.

Jamie was beginning to realize that there were some kinds of seeds inside him starting to ripen, and that girls were something more than other kids who went to separate washrooms. He blushed easily, and one little filly who sat directly behind him seemed to be charging her batteries every day by making his face turn as red as the sweater he had brought from Quagmire at wholesale.

Mother Benton advised her boys that the best way to avoid trouble was to join the Tuxis Boys at the Methodist Church and find friends there. Bob took her advice. He entered into all of the programs relating to fitness and vigour. At home, his KYBO chart was kept up so religiously that Louisa Benton was moved to ask what it was all about. In the category designated "Keep Your Bowels Open" he had chalked up an impressive record, but he had also searched out a robust ally for other endeavours. He made friends with a well-muscled lad who worked at the butcher shop after school lifting meat carcasses around. If he could lift a side of beef, Bob reasoned, he would have no trouble helping him flatten out an adversary.

This all happened during the first term. They had learned to keep boots clean in order not to be called "stubble jumpers." They had established a routine in doing home studies. Bob had moved up one grade in high school and so had Norman. Jamie was in the entrance grade now. Mrs. Benton was satisfied that they were starting to "get civilized," so she now felt better about going back to work in the Quagmire store as they had planned.

About ten days after the new term started, housing arrangements at Burdock took another twist. While at classes, Norman and Bob made the acquaintance of two other boys coming in from "the sticks." Carl Ericson came from a farm at Wood Mountain, near the Montana border, and John Blaney's people lived about six miles south of town— just far enough to make driving to school a nuisance. They were looking for a place to stay and they knew kindred souls when they met them. So, after a few talk sessions and a visit to the Benton shack, a bargain was struck.

The plan was simple, and not unique to prairie dwellers either: Carl and John would bunk at the shack, contributing farm produce such as vegetables, eggs and meat. The Benton cow would supply the milk, and the chore of milking would be shared. The Quagmire store would provide such items as sugar, salt, canned goods and blankets. Laundry would be taken home on weekends, and the general housing chores would be shared by all. The agreement would be taken to the home establishment for ratification and, if accepted, tenancy would commence in two weeks.

When Bill Benton was confronted with the proposition, he agreed in principle but added some provisos. During the previous term, a glassed-in verandah had been built onto the front of the building. The new contract called for a cellar to be dug under the back part of the house in preparation for the building of a lean-to kitchen. The household would be supplied with picks and shovels and given three weeks to complete the excavation.

Well, the digging enterprise was completed on schedule. The following week a Norwegian carpenter arrived to put up the framework, install all windows and put on the roof. Norman Benton was to supervise the completion of interior work and the cleanup. The "country hicks" were given a chance to show their mettle, and they rather relished the role.

No kitchen, of course, is complete without a flat-topped range, so Norman went to the closest auction yard, taking Carl Ericson along as advisor. They bought a McClary Good Cheer range together with attached hot-water reservoir and stove pipes to connect with the chimney. It would sit near the centre of the room with a woodbox pushed behind and against the wall. Woodboxes held the firewood, but they also acted as a catch-all for waste scraps of lumber and sometimes a hiding place for the coal scuttle.

To complete the inventory, Bill Benton sent up a big oak barrel. True, it had once been filled with linseed oil, but the taste wouldn't last forever, and it had a good lid. Every Monday morning, old Joe Gorst drove past with a tank of drinking water, and the rate was five cents per pail. A punched ticket hanging on a nail behind the stove kept the score.

When it came to the other "essential services," they decided that something a little more advanced than the two-holer at the back of the lot would be desirable, particularly in winter. So, at a location that was accessible to all rooms in the place, they established an enclosed compartment, elevated somewhat off the floor and equipped with a metal container with a hinged seat which could be kept under sanitary control through the use of generous treatments of chloride-of-lime. Jamie referred to this special compartment as the "poop-deck." Every Saturday morning (usually during the breakfast meal) a rather quaint character whom everybody called Uncle Hank arrived at the door with his "honey wagon," made a direct thrust through the kitchen, scooped up his prize in the poop-deck, and carried it to his waiting vehicle on the street. Hank was a taciturn sort who spoke little but whistled continuously. His wry sense of propriety was symbolized by a drinking cup that dangled from a hook at the back of his tank.

Rumour had it that his salary was just a level higher than the principal at Burdock High.

And that pretty well completed the list of essential services needed to start the new term. There were three beds, a couch, five chairs, a table, a cast-iron frying pan, some assorted cooking gear, and five young prairie hopefuls who knew how to ride horses but had never seen a streetcar, skin a rabbit but not a tourist, play a game but not for keeps. They had investigated the ravines and the coulees. Now came the world.

The place where the cow was finally tethered was a good mile from the house. The location had been scouted out and seemed ideal—down past the grain elevators, over the railroad tracks near the C.P.R. roundhouse. A reservoir dam had been built there to assure a supply of water for the engines and to fill a reserve storage tank. Clumps of bulrushes skirted the dam itself, with a few muskrat huts among the reeds at the shallow end. Norman thought that the cow would be content among all the greenery, and Bob was aware that muskrat pelts sometimes sold for two or three dollars each in season.

When it came to production, Daisy the cow, did her share. There was always more milk than they could drink, so some customers were supplied at ten cents per quart. In order to keep the milk money coming in, the boys took turns at milking—one went in the morning and another rode a bicycle to the site after school. With a little bit of luck, the evening rider could peddle over, milk Daisy, move the tethering stake to greener pasture and be back in time for supper—depending, of course, on who wore the cook's hat that night. With Carl in charge of the skillet, it was assured that food would be plain and the quantities immense. John liked to putter and experiment.

This week, Jamie and Norman were off duty, but fully engaged in a project of their own in the open field on the opposite side of the street.

When the travelling circus had set up in Burdock the previous week, all five of the lads had been on deck to gaze at the great wonders. To their way of thinking, it was a display of such splendour that they could hardly stop dreaming. As a matter of fact, that's what Norman and Jamie were doing over in the field—they were erecting a trapeze.

Two telephone poles, about eight feet apart, were already standing firmly erect. An iron pipe was threaded through two holes at the top and from it hung two long ropes with iron rings dangling about six feet off the ground. This was to be the new headquarters for aspiring gymnasts, even though nobody knew anything about the art.

Neighbours wondered what was going on, but kids began to gather there every evening after supper like moths drawn to a porch light.

As a trapeze performer, surprisingly enough, young Jamie became the envy of all the young fry in the area. Kids said he was "double jointed," but Bob claimed that he got more practice because he didn't know how to milk a cow.

In spite of this contention, however, Jamie persisted and improved. He did twirls, difficult manoeuvres where his shoulders appeared to come loose from their sockets, and he hung precariously from the toes of one foot. Kids from all over the neighbourhood came to watch and try out their own specialties, and among them was Millie Patrick, who came from a large family of harum-scarum kids down the street. There was also Cliff Bodner, who had dropped out of school and owned a motorcycle. Cliff had a job at the local planing mill where they made window sashes, and he claimed to be making eighteen dollars a week. Bob was one of the two kids allowed on Cliff's motorcycle. The other was Millie.

One Saturday, about the time Bob was getting ready to go on his milking mission, the big machine pulled up and Cliff sat there smiling.

"Why don't you climb aboard and I'll take you over to your cow," he suggested. "It beats riding on that thing."

Bob didn't like the inference concerning his bike, but when Cliff explained that he could hold one pail in each hand for balance, he thought he'd give it a try. He had hardly taken up position behind Cliff on the seat when the big Harley took off in a cloud of dust. They went down Fifth Avenue to the roundhouse road, followed a path across the pasture field where the cow was grazing, hit the accelerator, blew the horn and skidded in sideways to a spectacular stop. Well, it was a good circus act, but Bob was scared out of his wits and old Daisy was so disturbed that she retaliated in the only way a cow can—she refused to let down her milk. Bob coaxed, rubbed milk veins and stripped, but two skimpy quarts seemed to be the total offering. Daisy was holding it back for a more understanding approach to her favours.

The return trip was a disaster as well. Travelling over bumps with a quart of precious milk in each hand would constitute a good balancing act in itself, but reasonable discretion was sadly lacking. Bob knew that the two quarts might satisfy the regular customers, but he also knew that there would be no milk for breakfast and that he would be the one to take the blame. He made up his mind that, in the future, if Cliff Bodner wanted to take anybody for a ride on his thrill machine, he could take Millie.

112

The ride resulted in a cooling of relationships, but that didn't stop Cliff from showing up occasionally at the trapeze. One time he told Bob that he was going to take Millie out to the fairgrounds and see if she would like to "jazz." He said that her sister did and Millie was sixteen now. Somehow the subject seemed distasteful to Bob, so he let it drop. In the back of his mind the words of Louisa Benton kept interjecting themselves—words to the effect that a young fellow could get all the social life he needed at the Methodist Young Peoples' Club.

So that Thursday night Bob went to the Club and got acquainted with an older boy who was in Grade Twelve. He was studying biology, he said, and he seemed to know quite a bit about mammals and insects and reptiles. He said they had to dissect frogs in class and had to be able to name their parts. Of course, these interests found a kindred soul in the boy from Quagmire who had vast experiences with skunks and coyotes, so Richard Kean seemed certainly a good type to cultivate. Richard was from a farm just on the outskirts of town. His father had cattle and some saddle horses. You didn't run into fellows like that too often, so Bob launched out with a series of questions that might cement the friendship—such vital questions as, can you braid square using rawhide laces? Do you have a collection of animal skulls? Can you ride bareback like an Indian while you spin a rope? All of these questions, of course, he himself could answer in the affirmative.

Well, Richard was indeed a kindred soul. He said that such questions indicated the working of a "keen mind." He explained to Bob that when you get to Grade Twelve there are so many new subjects to learn about that nobody can get it all from school books. His big source, he said, was by ordering a great number of titles from the series of Little Blue Books published by J.E. Haldeman-Julius in the States. You could get them for ten cents each and they'd come in the mail.

Richard said that once he had read *The Mansions of Philosophy* by Will Durant, but he didn't quite understand it all. Even so, Bob was impressed. Richard added that his current reading was a Little Blue Book called *Religious Thoughts in Other Places*, which dealt with "comparative religions," whatever that was.

Bob was somewhat nonplussed with all this complicated talk. He had started off with frogs and coyotes and ended up with comparative religion. However, this was his chance to become an intellectual like Richard, so he certainly shouldn't slack off in his interest. The moment of decision came when Richard issued an invitation. There would be a revival meeting next Wednesday night on a farm near their place where the Holy Rollers were going to save sinners. It would be a fine opportunity to hear what was being said by this particular group of "fundamentalists." Would he like to go?

There was no question of acceptance. This would certainly be a better pastime than scaring cows with a motorcycle and cutting off the milk revenue.

When Wednesday evening came, Bob ate his supper quickly and rode his bike out to the Kean farm. The buildings were nicely painted and surrounded by a windbreak of Manitoba maples. The two boys met and, without taking time for introductions to parents, or saying anything about going to the revival meeting, climbed onto two saddle horses and rode off without ceremony.

"Be sure you hombres are back for breakfast," Mr. Kean called as they passed through the gate.

About a half-hour later, when they drew rein to enter a farmyard about three miles away, it was to find that the yard was already full of vehicles, horses tied to buggy-wheels and people congregating around a roped-off area protected from the wind by a huge implement shed.

There was a pulpit arrangement set on a wooden platform at the front, and chairs set out to accommodate the choir at the back. Rows of plank benches were almost full, while around the platform a bed of wheat-straw lay on the ground about twelve inches deep. As the boys worked their way over to the roped-off section, the choir was singing "Count Your Many Blessings" with such fervour that faces were wreathed in smiles. Neighbours nodded to one another in recognition as they passed to the remaining seats.

From the location he had chosen by the ropes, Richard viewed the proceedings and turned to his younger friend. "Religious ritual," he explained, "seems to be something that is found among all people of the world. When they have had good fortune or good crops, they think they should be thankful to somebody, or some force."

Bob couldn't quite understand what all this had to do with wheat-straw, but he was prepared to wait.

"You can read about primitive tribes up the Zambezi River. They hold festivals in the jungle after they have gathered in a season's food supply," Richard went on, "and they are doing essentially the same thing here."

To Bob, that sure sounded interesting. He thought that Richard must have quite a vast knowledge to know what was going on up the Zambezi River. However, and before he had time to give it much more thought, two men went up to the pulpit, and one of them was introducing "Evangelist Billie Bender—reformed drunkard and gambler who has just come to us with a message of love and hope."

The Reverend Bender didn't lose much time in getting the service underway. Pumping with great vigour, the organist struck up the first chord and a recently rehearsed assortment of stringed instruments launched into the first chorus of "Little Brown Church in the Wildwood" with a special drum treatment when they broke for the special "come! come! come! come!" interlude.

The uplifting lilt of the music was something that Bob had never witnessed at church services in Quagmire—and who had ever heard of guitars in church? He was pondering this aspect of the revival mood, when an accordion duet elevated "There's Joy in the Blood of the Lamb" to a rousing crescendo. It was a dramatic moment and the Reverend Bender did not miss the chance to continue the momentum.

With arms aloft, he first brought the crowd to a moment of complete silence. His voice commenced in low register, giving thanks in solemn tones for all of the bounty from the fields. Then he elaborated on the blessings of a bumper crop of flax on the newly broken sod, and stepped up the tempo with mention of how the Lord had got the turkeys to clean all the grasshoppers out of the oats when it was in the shot blade, and ended up with a personal endorsement of Red Fife wheat. The special spirit of joy and happiness that abounded at chicken-supper time, he said, had a spiritual quality transcending the manufactured square-dance fun in the school houses. But when he bore down on the purpose to which the rye crop had been put, his fist came down on the pulpit and his attack on the "forces of sin" was launched in earnest.

"Brothers, I sank into the deepest pits of mire!" he proclaimed. "Into the slime, with the grasping claws of satan clutching for my whisky-saturated soul!!"

And with these words, the Reverend Billie led into a confessional that dragged his tortured body through the gambling dens of Sudbury, into the flop-houses of Toronto and Winnipeg, and even to the flesh-pots of gangster-ridden Chicago. From what he said, Rip Hogan and his crowd at the Quagmire livery barn were a fraternity of angels.

The confessional came to a simmering conclusion, followed directly by a call for prayers and supplication for "all those who have sinned and lost their way."

For a moment Bob did a little reflecting on his own behaviour. Was there something that he had swept under the rug and should now drag out for closer scrutiny? There had been times that he had lingered on the edge of an act or a thought that might be construed as a mini-sin, but he wasn't sure that his transgressions would rate in the same league with what went on in Chicago, or even Sudbury. He certainly had never had to struggle with a whisky-saturated soul.

The choir was softly singing "Blessed Redeemer, Jesus Is Mine" when Richard caught his eye. "I wonder if the primitive tribes have any flesh-pots quite as spicy as the ones in Chicago?" Richard whispered. The inference passed right over Bob's head. He was listening intently to the music.

The Reverend Billie was now singing along with the choir and boosting his upturned palms in rising swells in order to induce more fervour. The crowd responded. Then, as the last words of the last stanza ended, he stepped forward toward the roped-off area, looked searchingly at the crowd with words of entreaty on his lips. "Are there any of you here who are without sin?"

Nobody answered. Bob guessed they were all like him.

"Are there any of you tonight who are ready to repent and yield your souls to the Saviour?" was the next query. Yes, it looked as though all of those iniquities, large and small, would have to be dragged out into the open.

From that moment forth, the Reverend Billie regaled sin with deepening conviction. The music sang about "a home up yonder." The good pastor stalked the forces of evil and the choir burst forth with "Glory Road." Singly, and in small groups, a scattering of people were starting to move down the aisles.

"Won't you give your soul to the Lord tonight?" came the solemn entreaty. "Another soul for the Master," he acknowledged, patting an elderly lady on the shoulder as she passed. "Won't you come? Won't you come *NOW?*"

The "amens" were coming from all quarters of the congregation.

On their knees in the straw, with arms stretched to the heavens, twenty to thirty supplicants were now into a more advanced state of spiritual enchantment. The night was still, the music had risen to a new crescendo and bodies were swaying to the rhythm. Some were making strange jabbering noises that Bob had never heard come out of mortals before. Others held both hands aloft and were trembling like loose shingles in a high wind. In a far corner, and settled deep in the straw, Bob thought he could recognize Mrs. Kuplinski, the same lady who had killed his pet coyote with a neck-yoke the year before, just because it was eating her chickens.

"Do you think they put on a better show up the Zambezi River?" Richard inquired. "Possibly more drums and feathers, eh?"

Bob just smiled and kept an attentive eye on the proceedings.

Directly in front of where they stood, a portly woman who had been supporting her trembling arms in the air for about fifteen minutes, suddenly toppled over and started rolling about. Her gingham dress was long, but it kept billowing above her knees and pretty soon a pair of generous-sized bloomers came into view.

Bob was taken aback for the moment. He couldn't believe his eyes. But Richard was solemnly reading the faded inscription across her ample bottom—"ROBIN HOOD FLOUR—For Household Use." Even the marksman, with drawn bow, appeared to be standing guard.

A display of undergarments like that, Bob thought, would be considered a shameful thing at Quagmire. It seemed that the only Christian thing for him to do was to lend a helping hand, so he reached over the ropes when he thought nobody was looking, and was about to pull the dress back to a respectable position, when he heard a voice.

"Stand back, son, let her glory shine." The Reverend Bender was waiting nearby and tapping his hand with a director's stick.

That was enough for Bob. He felt humiliated. He wanted to vanish into thin air. When he saw the look on Richard's face, he knew the feeling was mutual.

Ten minutes later they rode along the country road discussing the whole affair. Richard speculated that the people were "hypnotized" when they made all those jabbering noises.

"They call it 'speaking in tongues'," he explained. "But some medical doctors claim that extra adrenalin is pumped into the bloodstream when they are in an emotional state, and that's what keeps their motors 'revved up' so high."

When the two researchers arrived at the Kean farm, they put the horses away and had a glass of cold milk. Bob rode home on his bike in a state of confusion. He didn't know whether he was interested in comparative religion or not.

At school the next morning, Bob could hardly get the revival meeting out of his mind. An even greater conundrum was what to make of Richard Kean. With an interest in such disturbing subjects, would he make a desirable friend? He had read the Little Blue Book that Richard had given him and was interested in what Mohammed, Buddha and Zoroaster meant to the people of Asia, but what did that have to do with the Holy Rollers in the Burdock district? At times Richard seemed to be making light of them. Sure, he was a member of the Young Peoples' Club at the Methodist Church, but was this interest in comparative religion more of a hazard than Cliff Bodner and his motorcycle?

Bob wished he could find a friend that he could really understand—someone like his old pal Gordon Didgey. He had heard a rumour that Gordon might be coming to Burdock right after harvest to stay with his aunt and attend the same high school. He hoped the rumour was true.

Friday, at the dinner table, both Carl and John announced that they would be going home to the country as soon as school disbanded for the weekend. Jamie and Norman had announced that they, too, were going to Quagmire. It was the time of year when the wild creatures are scurrying about, gathering in their own harvest for winter. The eight-mile hike down the railway track would take about two hours, and they could be home for a "decent meal." It was Bob's turn to stay and look after the place, so it was up to him to settle down and make his own plans. Of course, old Daisy would have to be looked after and the extra milk delivered. Then he could heat up a couple of eggs with some beans for a meal. Buster Keaton was playing at the Mustang Theatre and the kids said he was a real nutty character, so he could go there.

But it was hard to get away from the neighbourhood that night. After a makeshift meal, Bob noticed a collection of kids at the trapeze. There was a lot of laughing and kibbitzing going on, so he thought that it might be a good time to wander over and try some of the new stunts he had learned. Jamie wouldn't be there to steal his thunder, so he could indulge in a little bit of showing off.

As he approached, a fat kid from the restaurant was hanging from one leg and pretending he was an opera singer upside down, while the young fry stood around and giggled. An overgrown Airedale pup jumped and lolled with some kids on the grass. Two grade-eighters from down the street were waiting their turn on the trapeze while a harum-scarum quartet of brats ran in and out playing touched-you-last.

Bobby was pleased indeed when, on his approach, much of the frivolity came to a stall. Somehow, he thought, it showed that they knew he was one of the "owners." It was very pleasant to feel this kind of adulation, but there was a temporary distraction as he noticed Millie Patrick sauntering up the road. She came walking along at a leisurely pace, tossing the mass of black hair over her shoulder and singing softly to herself.

Young Bob had never talked to her alone when Cliff wasn't around. She was a little bit skinny, and she always wore tight skirts. She had a pleasant smile. And the firm little bumps that were developing under her blouse didn't go without notice, either. He remembered what Cliff had said about going to the fairgrounds sometime.

"You're late tonight," he ventured. "Your boyfriend gave up and went home, I guess."

Millie leaned against the trapeze post and crossed her legs, standing on one foot. "What makes you think he's my boyfriend?" she quipped with a breezy air.

Bob blushed. He could feel goose bumps all up the back of his neck. He couldn't think of anything to say.

At his feet, a sniffly-nosed Mullins kid was pulling on his arm. The other kids called him Kayo and his principle attention-getter today was the six stitches he had to exhibit from having fallen off a water tank. But who cared about stitches? Certainly not Bob. The rings were temporarily abandoned now, so he leaped into the air, seized them on the back swing and did a revolving manoeuvre that he had not even dreamed of accomplishing before. Like the guy in the circus, he did two complete loops through the air, dropping to his feet directly in front of Millie, and stood puffing. By this time his face was so red that nobody could tell whether it was blood pressure or blushing.

"It's your turn now," he challenged. "Can I help you up?"

Millie needed no coaxing. She leaped off the ground, swung low on the first pass, and then executed a full somersault with thighs, underpants and everything else showing. His challenge had been met with interest.

But after such a display of prowess and bare flesh, Bob's mind started to do some strange gymnastics all of its own. The other boys had all gone home for the weekend and the house was empty. The chores had all been completed and he didn't really have to see Buster Keaton. Possibly Millie would hang around 'til all the little kids went home and then they could get better acquainted. It was a deliciously dangerous thought that entered his mind, got chucked out once or twice, and then was taken back to be entertained further.

It was during one of these moments of turmoil that old lady Keeler called her brood to come home to bed. Others took this as a cue and started wending their way across the vacant lot toward the houses. Each evacuation seemed to quicken the tempo of Bob's pulse. As the moments ticked on, more mothers called their kids and others drifted away. They had got down to the last holdout, and Millie was still there.

The later it got, the more the inner compulsion grew. It was like trying to hold the lid on the teakettle when all of the drafts on the stove were full open. By this time he couldn't even speak to her. He just walked past and hoped that she'd say something that he could pick up and add to. But she didn't. She just stood there with head cocked to one side and wearing a smile which Bob interpreted as the deepest of female intuition.

Finally he realized that it was now or never. Wrong or right, win or lose, he must do something. The next swing past on the trapeze, he stopped abruptly before Millie and with an absurd grin blurted out his question. "How would you like to jazz?"

Well, you couldn't get a much more straightforward question than that. Nor could you be much blunter. He stood teetering on his feet and the echo of the words was still reverberating through his cranium when Millie turned on her heels and took off like a gazelle. The last glimpse he got of her was when she jumped the fence and disappeared into the big frame house in the second block down the street.

It was as though the bottom had fallen out of everything. Nothing was working out. It was too early to go to bed, too late to go to the show, and an entire evening in a vacant house locked up with his conscience lay before him. Thoughts of the Reverend Billie Bender started to skitter through his mind, and he wondered if any revivalist would be interested in recruiting a number one wet-behind-the-ears sinner. He was either a sinner or a chump. He didn't quite know which.

Across the street, the Benton shack was in complete darkness. Bob was glad. He knew he could slink across the road, turn the knob on the door, and he needn't emerge until daylight.

The lock snapped shut, and he was alone with the four walls.

The first antidote, of course, was to try to banish the whole sordid affair from his mind by reading a book. One of the Little Blue Books with the intriguing title *Religious Thoughts in Far Off Places* came immediately to hand, but when the cover fell back, it opened on a chapter entitled, "The Strange Mating Rituals of the Hottentots." From there he turned to the gramophone records and played "The Rose of Picardi" three times, ending up with "The Little Rosewood Casket" and the complete works of Harry Lauder. He drank three cups of hot chocolate and ate half a pound of bologna. At ten o'clock, this boy from Quagmire climbed into bed with a full stomach and a scrambled mind.

Bob's bedroom was against the west wall and had one window facing the sidewalk, a small door leading to the "poop deck" and another door opening into the kitchen. As he lay looking up at the ceiling, he was conscious of every tick of the kitchen clock from ten until midnight. Insomniacs say that in two hours, a ticking clock will either drive a person bonkers or put them to sleep. In this case, slumber claimed the body, but dreaming took up the slack in his mental processes.

It would be difficult to say how many times, in his dreams, he turned up at the Holy Roller meeting and then managed to escape. The Reverend Billie kept driving his point about sin and adultery, and at one time almost skewered him with his black conductor's stick, demanding that he repent and be saved. And every time he arrived at the threshold of redemption, Richard Kean seemed to turn up and remind him about the rituals up the Zambezi River. The dream went on and on, aided and abetted by the bologna, until some time after one o'clock he passed into some sort of suspended animation.

Then, in the quiet of night, there came a knock on the window-pane. At first it seemed like a dim faraway message by telegraph. Then it came louder and subsided, only to return again.

In a moment the frightened teenager was awake and bolt upright. Someone was definitely there and determined to get in that window. Possibly somebody thought the inhabitants had all gone home for the weekend and was trying to burglarise the place? Possibly someone looking for John or Carl? In any case, they were trying to see if the sash would pry loose. Who would be doing that?

Bob considered calling out, but that would reveal his location. It was better to sit in the dark and ponder the possibilities. Suppose Millie had gone home and told her father? Suppose he was a red-headed Irishman and had come to skin him alive? These were the most tantalizing thoughts of all.

The knocking on the window subsided and then resumed at the back door this time. Bob could hear the screen door being unlatched. Someone was fooling with the lock.

The time for action was close. The beleaguered one slipped on his pants and shirt, sneaked into the kitchen and filled a pail to the brim with water from the big barrel behind the door. At a chosen moment, he would release the lock and fling the door wide open. In a split second the assailant would have to be recognized as either friend or foe or stranger. If it was Millie's father, he would most certainly get doused with cold water and, while he was sputtering, Bob would escape between his legs into the street. At the shed, he could grab his bike and hit for the open spaces.

The moment of decision was *NOW!*

He flung the door open so wide that it crashed against the wall with a bang, and there, facing him in complete bewilderment, stood his mother—Louisa Benton in the flesh!!

While driving through Quagmire earlier in the day, a friend from

Burdock had offered her a ride to town and Louisa had seized upon the opportunity, looking forward to a full Saturday of shopping in the larger stores. She knew that Bob had been left to hold the fort, and so he was. She just couldn't understand why he could not hear her banging.

The five-cent pail of water was returned to the barrel unused. Emotions quickly simmered back to normal. A towering load of care melted away from Bob's social sensibilities. He never confessed his "sin" to anybody.

In truth, it was all just part of the process of higher education at Burdock, Saskatchewan.

10

ALL A QUESTION OF GLANDS

*A*LL in all, the quest for higher education was a battle that afforded little time for introspection. It was a case of making the best of every situation and never ask for quarter. Throughout the country there were ominous signs of economic paralysis; for the Saskatchewan prairie, where there had already been crop failure, there was no use kidding any longer.

That summer the Benton boys used every opportunity to forage afield, scouting the countryside for jobs of any description. They worked on farms, ranches and on the roads. Bob and his friend Gordon Didgey took a contract to re-shingle the roof of the C.P.R. station at Quagmire. Norman learned to braid tails and manes in prospect of finding work decorating stallions for show at fall fairs. Carl Ericson's father taught him how to splice rope, thinking that there would be a small demand for these services at the grain elevators when aging rope-pulley systems kept wearing out and funds were limited to buy new equipment. On one occasion, Jamie and Bob worked as clerk and flunky for an auctioneer, where junk had to be sorted and listed for auction. Nobody could say that they lacked resourcefulness.

Even when school reconvened in the fall, some of the connections with summer employment were kept alive, like Bob's association with the auctioneer, for example. He found great fascination in sorting through bric-a-brac, rusty trinketry of yesterday, and even the dog-eared books that still carried the haunting smells of history. That possibly explained why the Benton shack accumulated such a wide assortment of literature—editions on American criminology, new studies in gynecology and methods of child delivery, a volume dealing with life in Tanganyika, books on how to read palms, a collection of stamps from Somaliland and one slightly used boomerang, said to have been the former property of a genuine Australian aborigine.

The matter of saving fuel was another department where economies could be effected. There were no water tap to freeze, so cold temperatures at night posed no threat. Jamie and Bob read and swallowed whole every word in *Physical Culture Magazine*, and consequently insisted on sleeping in the glassed-in verandah even at extreme temperatures. Technique, they claimed, was the whole secret, and they followed a procedure that read something like the recipe for coddled kippers. First you stoke up the stove in the parlour to the point where the paint is almost blistered off the ceiling. During this period, throw two cats under blankets in bed, positioning cats where backs of sleepers will eventually be resting. After having pulled on flannelette pajamas, throw doors of verandah wide open for three minutes; then leap into bed and locate cats. Pull blankets over head leaving only a hole for breathing and have a third party cover entire bed with quilt or buffalo robe if available. Leave to simmer.

On one occasion they slept blissfully through a howling blizzard and awoke to find a drift of snow piled across the foot of their bed. Some measures, of course, were fun, but they did not blind the boys to noticing contrasts with some other homes in the community. One family of Metis used a tent on moderate nights to accommodate the overflow numbers in their family, but there were other students in their classes who lived in brick houses with furnaces in the basement. The Bentons were glad that they had learned to tough it out, but there was still the compelling need to cut down on expenses.

And, as if being resourceful and frugal was not enough, fate at just this time dealt them another blow. Word came through one day that their father, Bill Benton, had been struck down in a fatal accident.

Numb with grief, Louisa Benton and her three teenagers gratefully accepted the solace of sorrowing neighbours, eloquent eulogies, newspaper editorials and a huge prairie funeral.

Time slowly eased the pain of losing a well-loved father and husband. Louisa moved permanently to Burdock with the boys, and eventually future plans and new directions absorbed the family's thoughts as summer and fall passed quietly and the school term entered its final phase.

Christmas had sapped most of their financial reserves, and now ways had to be found to recoup these funds and, if possible, supply some simple luxuries. Socks and sweaters were all home-knit. Every avenue of saving was explored, but eventually it seemed that they would have to dig still deeper.

The "Help Wanted" section of the *Regina Leader-Post* carried its usual list of opportunities for people who wanted to make a career of porch-climbing and pushing sales on their neighbours, but this seemed so futile in a small town. Surely, Louisa Benton thought, it should be possible to find something more dignified. So, after some preliminary correspondence and deep contemplation, she decided to allow herself to be appointed the "District Corseteer" for the Spirella Foundation Co. of Winnipeg. The front room would be graced with her gilt-edged diploma, appropriately framed. It declared to all and sundry that she "had passed a rigorous course in the art of Body Moulding" and was "competent to advise and prescribe suitable garments for all those ladies who wish to recapture the scintillating symmetry of the feminine form."

The boys, too, were trying to do their part. Bob decided to scout out and extend his weasel trapline. On Saturday mornings, he set out after breakfast, covered the fairgrounds area, a cut-bank on either side of the rail tracks, two farm properties and a frozen-over slough—about five square miles in all. So, at least there were two enterprises underway—fitting corsets and trapping weasels.

Then one day Louisa got another letter in the mail. It was from the Spirella people, and it told of the great profits that were just waiting out there for people who would make an effort to contact ladies of "more generous dietary indulgences during the Yuletide Feasts, and who would need a 'lift' at this time of the year." There were special price reductions for January selling and an additional ten percent incentive package for representatives who would really go "Full Out on the March down the Silver Trail to Greater Earnings."

The time had passed for skittish doubts. Louisa dug through her purse for the list of names she had compiled, went to the phone in the front room and after the first call, came back ecstatic.

"Mrs. Clinton Rhomer is coming over tomorrow night to be measured," she announced proudly. "Guess I should have called her sooner."

"She's a good one to get started on," Norman quipped. "If you can solve her problems of bulgy butt, there's all her cronies at the euchre club who need some help at uplift after sitting down so much."

Mrs. Benton ignored that remark and went right ahead with her promotional program. She got Mrs. Rhomer measured that Sunday and six other ladies the following week. "Sale'ing down the Silver Trail," like it said in the pamphlet, looked as if it might become a profitable voyage.

Most of the traffic came when the boys were at school, so there was no real confusion in the little house. Bob had started his trapline and went before breakfast twice a week. He had two weasels already to show for his efforts. The snow-white pelts were stretched over shingles cut to shape, every tail with the black tip attached. He was proud because that was the mark of an expert skinner.

The general picture was starting to brighten but, when supper was convened that Saturday night, Mrs. Benton had a special announcement to make.

"I was pleased to get ladies from the euchre club," she enthused, "but I didn't think that the aristocracy of the district would be interested in my services. Would you believe that Mrs. James Quigley is coming over for a fitting tomorrow afternoon? Isn't that something?"

"Well, you got the right one on the line that time," said Norman again. He seemed to have started to notice shapes more than the younger ones. "She was a good looker when she first married Jimmie, but she's got lumps growing on top of the other lumps now."

"And since when did you get on such close terms with James Quigley to be allowed to call him 'Jimmie'?" snapped Mrs. Benton. "As for his wife, it's not nice to speak disrespectfully of people who are putting bread on your table like that. Sometimes it's glands," she admonished.

Long before Mrs. Quigley arrived the following day, the place was prepared for her reception. An especially warm fire had been made in the front room, and the framed diploma was hung conspicuously above a small table covered with a lace runner and carrying a neatly arranged complement of measuring tapes, pins, samples and a style book with the words "Spirella Fashion Winners" lettered on the cover in gold.

Mrs. Quigley was no newcomer to Burdock. She had, during her maiden years, been crowned Miss Wheat Pool at the Swift Current Fair. Possibly that had gone to her head, because she stopped talking to the Burdock swains for almost a year, and then she married this fellow who was a district manager for the Imperial Oil Company in town. That was before she got the lumps.

Unfortunately, Bob was not able to be present when she made her entry to the Benton home that Sunday. He had left on his trapline early in the afternoon. In the interim, however, events at the Corset Salon were going according to plan. Norman, Jamie and Carl were all banished to the kitchen. When Mrs. Quigley rang the doorbell, Norman greeted her, took her coat, ushered her to an easy chair in the parlour and left to call the corseteer. Louisa then made her entry, the door closed behind her and Norman came back through the hallway carrying a fox-trimmed creation. Norman could have just hung the coat up with the rest of the jumbo-knit sweaters and mackinaw coats, but the overpowering potency of the perfume must have had an unbalancing effect on his own glands. When Bob suddenly arrived from his trek in the outdoors, he could easily have imagined he was stepping into a fashion salon in Creeds.

Norman, dressed in high-heeled pumps, was posing with a long-stemmed cigarette holder while he modeled a luxurious garment with red-fox collar. Behind him were two forms crouched by the keyhole leading to the front room and giving back sketchy reports with bulging eyeballs.

Bob was so taken aback with the sight that met his eyes that he dropped his bag and its contents on the kitchen floor and spent a few anxious moments wondering whether or not he should get implicated and possibly steal a look at the keyhole himself. After all, there was no charge.

Well, Louisa Benton had often tried to explain the phenomenon called "women's intuition" to her boys, but this time she must have been getting astrological vibrations simultaneously. Possibly she felt a draft from under the door—or possibly she recognized a familiar odour from the kitchen.

When Bob had dropped his bag on the floor, what he had forgotten in the excitement was its contents—two muskrat carcasses and a dead weasel. The animals had partially emptied some of their glandular excretions at the time they had been caught, and the warmth of the room had caused the vapours to become airborne. Convection currents were now carrying the message to other parts of the house.

Mrs. Benton got to the door before her client realized the full significance of what was transpiring. There was one mad scramble in the kitchen, with three turkey-toms temporarily jammed in the doorway. The fox-collared coat was thrown in a heap on the top shelf of the closet, and the exodus continued through the door of the back porch into the yard with a bag of smelly varmints leading the way.

During the remainder of the fitting, Louisa Benton retained her composure although she found it almost painful to restrain a feeling of fermenting outrage. She explained that there must have been a skunk or something in the neighbourhood, and that the back door had blown open after the boys had gone out into the yard to check.

After the fitting, with Mrs. Quigley on her way, the scene was just a little different. Louisa declared that the clowns in the kitchen should be skinned alive for bringing her business to the perilous brink of ruin, and that another scene like that could make them the laughing stock of Burdock.

Norman said that Mrs. Quigley "still wasn't in bad shape after all." Carl expressed the opinion that she "looked like a spavined walrus."

On one thing they could all agree, however—it was all a question of glands.

11

THE TIME OF
THE BIG BLOW

WHEN the Quigley episode finally blew over, everybody settled down to some serious thinking. Louisa Benton had done well with her promotional work, and Norman had found work on weekends at the local Sash and Door Factory. But toward spring the prospect list of corset customers was badly depleted, and the Silver Trail had become an overgrown footpath. The time had come for some new avenues of endeavour.

On his rambles through the countryside, Bob had learned that a big marsh south of town was now in the melt stage and that muskrats, living in the bank of an abandoned road-grade, were now starting to move about. Gordon Didgey was able to borrow a horse and buggy from his uncle, so they decided to go there two or three times each week in order to visit a string of traps. By the middle of April, they had about ninety-five pelts hanging on drying frames. At approximately two dollars per skin, Bob's share would help to keep the ship afloat for a little longer.

But as spring extended into summer, hopes for a normal crop again faded. Seeds that had been planted in cultivated soil germinated and got an initial boost from moisture left from the winter's snow, but there were no spring rains—only searing heat. Anything that survived this stage was assailed by the usual pests such as hungry rodents nipping off tender shoots at the edge of the fields, but there was a new scourge as well. Grasshoppers had started to appear in clouds. On a bright day, people would congregate holding up shards of coloured glass against the sun's glare to see the extent of the infestation. It was not hard to determine where the particular cloud was located, for one could watch its shadow moving across the hillside. When the sloughs dried up, the birds could not drink, so they left the country and the grasshoppers had no enemies except man. Man seemed helpless. The first years of crop failure had been thought of as a test of mettle for the prairie people, but this was forewarning of a deadly, numbing disaster.

Some farmers from the Burdock district just called it quits. Some deserted their holdings and went back to eastern Canada. Some loaded all of their earthly belongings onto rickety wagons and headed for the Peace River country; brush had to be cut, scrub cleared and fields stoned, but at least there were homesteads to claim and a reprieve from dust and grasshoppers. It was worth the gamble.

This was also the year that Carl Ericson and young Bob would be writing their graduation exams in Burdock—senior matriculation, they called it then. The year was crucial, for it meant not only the end of a learning program, but final preparations for the great opportunities awaiting in the world without. And, as it happened, the word "without" was appropriate indeed.

By this time Norman had concluded that, being the oldest, the time had come for him to find permanent work in order to keep food on the table. He was able to convert his part-time status at the Sash and Door Factory to permanent employment. Jamie, who had had previous experience at keeping and accounting for stock, went down to the C.P.R. siding one Saturday with Gordon Didgey and was put to work on cars of relief goods arriving from the Maritimes and Ontario. The job was to sort out the bags of potatoes and turnips, count packages of cheese and tally up the tins of plum-and-apple jam. Every family in a long waiting line had to get a fair share, and it took real diplomacy to best satisfy the need. It wasn't much of a job, but Louisa Benton felt that the little ration Jamie brought home was pay for services rendered.

During this time, young Bob was plying the downtown section for job possibilities. In due course an opportunity presented itself at A.J. Feldman and Company, the local department store. Because he had been brought up in a store, he would be of some use after school and full time Saturdays as assistant flunky and all-purpose sales hand. He was back in the retail business again, this time in the shoe department and around the men's wear counter—at least a step up from unpacking and counting eggs at Quagmire. As he told the family, "I sell pants. That's an essential service, good times or bad. You see, it's illegal to go without pants, so the business world will always need my services."

Was there a future in the retail business? Well, at Burdock High he was learning all about the laws of supply and demand. The textbooks told of the new vistas that would open up for enterprising souls; they explained the methods by which the magic of trade and commerce rewarded business acumen and hard work. In the book it all seemed so elementary and rational, but Saturdays' experience at the Feldman establishment posed doubts. Doors were slamming shut as fast as new ones were opening. Farm customers, possibly the hardest workers of all, were beginning to look like a procession of tramps. The hand-me-down regalia of even town kids told a story of scraping through in threadbare condition from one relief voucher to the next. It was hard for many to look anything but gaunt on sorgum molasses and barley coffee, but they could still grin and show spunk.

One day Bob was tending his clothing counter at Feldman's when a dishevelled old woman appeared at the front door looking like a dyspeptic gopher that had just crawled through a culvert after a bad storm. In one hand she carried a tattered bag, in the other a rusty pail filled with eggs.

Without coming fully through the door, she directed an inquiry in a loud commanding voice. It was meant for the boss who was at the back of the store.

"Feldman," she shouted, "what are yez payin' fer eggs today?"

"I'm almost ashamed to tell you," Feldman answered in an apologetic voice. "The best we can do is ten cents a dozen."

The woman backed away and just before she slammed the door, her raspy voice cut the air in protest: "I'll take 'em home first! Ten cents don't pay fer the wear-'n-tear on the hen's asshole!!"

Bob was taken aback. He recognized the woman as Mrs. Abernethy, the same woman who had once brought the "prophesy egg" to the Benton store in Quagmire—the mystery egg with the numbers 1933 visible on the shell, an omen of the approaching Armageddon. He wondered if she was still fighting sin or whether she thought Armageddon had already arrived, and she was getting a little impatient for the final curtain to fall.

Hard times were exacting their toll, yet throughout the ordeal, the emphasis in the business world centred on the importance of salesmanship. Display windows showed "The Latest from the Fashion Centres of the World." An open display system of merchandising was introduced, where prospective customers would be able to see and feel the merchandise in order "to make a more intelligent choice of the many items available." Weekly advertisements in the *Burdock Bugle* urged people to "Take advantage of the wide selection available now," and "Choose from these many useful items." Choose? With what?

It was not unusual for whole families to congregate in the shoe department at Feldman's, occupy the seats and fitting stools and spend two or three hours trying to figure out how to make a sixty-dollar relief voucher stretch far enough to clothe six children so they could pull through the winter. The maximum they could spend on each item was stipulated on the back of each voucher and many times such prices were not obtainable. It disturbed young Bob deeply when many of these "family planning sessions" broke down in tears and disappointment.

On one occasion his will to promote sales with sufficient vigour seemed to be flagging and did not go unnoticed by his boss. A bit of a pep talk was in order. "You've got to get in there and sell," said Feldman. "Jack Andrews, who travels for Swift's, was to a sales seminar in Moose Jaw last week. Yesterday he told me he sold six cases of lunch tongue to stores down on the Mankota line where things are supposed to be at their worst."

"Fine," Bob countered. "When Jack Anderson dies some time, and appears before St. Peter to relate all of his accomplishments while on earth, he can proudly include the sale of six cases of lunch tongue at Mankota, Saskatchewan. That should get him direct passage to eternal bliss."

What was happening to him? Was he getting too snarky with his boss? Was he becoming a Bolshevik? He was often glad when the store closed and he could go home where there was some sense. He was certainly not finding it in the business world.

Out in the arena of perpetual struggle, it seemed that the aggressive types had the best chances of survival, but Louisa Benton had her own methods of keeping the ship afloat. She believed that the best way to face difficult times was with music. One day, while riding on the train to Moose Jaw, she met a lady music teacher who was attempting to establish classes of pupils in a clutch of small towns along the rail system. Well, it didn't take long for Louisa and Mrs. Bonnington to come to an understanding. The front room of the Benton house, where the piano now stood, would become a studio for two days of each week. Food, lodging and other social graces would be extended at no cost in exchange for free lessons for the Benton family. Everything was settled on the train; let the dance begin.

The following week, when Mrs. Bonnington arrived at her "conservatory" for the first tutoring session, she did not come alone. She said there might be some students in Burdock who would like to take some elocution lessons also, so she had taken the liberty of bringing along a younger sister, Miss Andrews, who was a graduate of the Philadelphia School of Expression. It certainly sounded impressive.

Without hesitation, Louisa Benton introduced the two newcomers to her male quartet and the rapport was instantaneous—Mrs. Bonnington was a positive personality, but her sister was a dish. The problem was one of mathematics. How do you fit seven adults into a shack with one bedroom, one parlour and one kitchen, even if it is only for two days and nights each week. Then, too, there would be the other students coming and going.

At first it didn't seem possible that these new additions could be properly accommodated, but there had been one oversight—the verandah. Norman and Carl could use the couch near the piano. The two guests could be offered the "boudoir"; Mrs. Benton could fix a bunk in the kitchen; Bob and Jamie would go to the verandah with the cat. Everything was settled.

Now came the matter of allocating lessons. Who had the talent and ambition to become musicians? Who had the aptitude for "expression," whatever that was? Putting it another way, who wanted to jazz it up and who wanted to ham it up? That didn't take long to decide, either—Norman and Jamie were enrolled as possible pianists because they had a liking for instrumental music. Carl and Bob chose elocution because they were infatuated with Miss Andrews.

For the remainder of the year there was joy in the Benton bivouac. Some funds came in from the Feldman department store, there was a full pay cheque earned at the Sash and Door Factory, corsets were sold from Monday to Wednesday, and a variety of pupils traipsed in and out of the "conservatory" during Friday and Saturday. Strains of "Robin's Return" floated on the early summer air together with Rimski-Korsakov's "Flight of The Bumblebee"; *The Shooting of Dan McGrew* vied in popularity with *Rubaiyat of Omar Khayyam*.

Even after the scheduled time of lessons, there was music and drama. During these hours of relaxation and approaching bedtime, there were often moments of outright hilarity. Mrs. Bonnington was a heavily bosomed woman whose whole frame fairly undulated when she laughed. Her sister had big blue picture-window eyes which she used with devastating effect, both in pursuit of literary expression, and to send gushes of adrenalin coursing through the veins of her adolescent admirers. One night, in that hour just before retirement, frivolities got to the stage of a garment-for-garment disrobement contest around the kitchen table, with Louisa ringing the bell when it got to the brassiere and underwear stage. This was certainly a new departure in the learning process, one that Louisa thought the boys needed, having never lived in a household with sisters of their own.

Weeks passed and every day was made to account for some progress. School homework was intense at the beginning of each week in order to allow for a more pleasant and exciting finale. There seemed to be an awakening interest in the performing arts generally. True, there was hardly an audience that did not still have to endure a few verses of *The Habitant Farmer*, *The Cremation of Sam Magee* or *Albert and the Lion*. But they also had the privilege to listen to stirring renditions of the latest Hollywood hits played by a clutch of Burdock instrumentalists with tinkling piano, moaning saxophones and lilting violins. But the town people were beginning to notice. What pinnacles of cultural attainment were scaled in that prairie domicile?

Early in the game, Norman Benton had found that, because of some strange wiring in his nervous hookup, he could not play piano. The fingers on his right hand always moved in unison with fingers on the left, and so could never be induced to play separate parts. Mrs. Bonnington, accordingly, switched him over to playing trumpet, where only one hand was necessary for fingering. In later concerts, the lad who did the fancy double-tongue bits in the solos was usually the lad from the Sash and Door Factory—and he was getting invitations to play in dance bands. Gordon Didgey showed great promise on the violin. Carl Ericson took a lead role in a three-act play staged at the Mustang Theatre and local news stories began to appear in the *Regina Leader* under the by-line of Robert Benton.

As the middle of June approached that summer, there might have been room for some concern, for that was graduation year for two from the Benton household. Had there been too much music? Too much hilarity and downright tomfoolery? Not aboard Louisa Benton's ship. She made the rules and stayed at the wheel. There was time for music, time for fun, and time for study, too. To graduate from high school into a competitive world was the best gift she could bestow on her sons. Young Bob was the first to be launched from the dock. Six weeks later, when the matriculation graduates were listed in the *Regina Leader*, the names of Carl Ericson and Robert C. Benton were included. Mission accomplished.

~

There was rejoicing at the bivouac that night, but in a sense there was melancholy, too. Everybody knew that at this point their stream of life had come to some kind of watershed. Carl had already gone back to the family farm at Wood Mountain and an uncertain future in a bad, if not one of the worst, drought areas. The end of the school term had seen the end of the Bonnington conservatory and the Andrews school of expression. Termination of lessons at Burdock High meant that the student body would scatter and few matriculation graduates could even think of university because of the financial blockages. There was a deepening realization that a new phase in the struggle for survival was just beginning.

As on other occasions when problems seemed overpowering and there was a need to confer with somebody outside his own home, Bob Benton sought out his old friend Gordon Didgey. Since the carefree days in the coulee country at Quagmire, Bob considered Gordon even closer than a brother. The attachment of the early days had never flagged during their tussle with town life and the mind-bending exercises of high school mathematics, biology and science.

One morning Bob walked down the street and across the vacant lot to the home on Sunset Street, where the Didgeys now lived. If they couldn't solve any problems, at least they could listen to his new crystal set, for Gordon had been the first kid in Burdock to assemble a radio receiver and had extra earphones for a friend. Other times they had learned about Clarence Darrow and the Scopes Trial, and Gordon had the first copy of Darwin's *Voyage of The Beagle* in town. Or, in the evenings, there was Amos 'n Andy or an episode from *The Shadow*. Anything you wanted, you could get at Gordon's.

But this visit with Gordon Didgey was different. Many times they had pondered the prospects for their futures and wondered what particular niche they might fit in society. This time there seemed a fearful compulsion that some kind of an answer be found, at least on a preliminary basis.

Bob spent most of the day at the Didgey home. Gordon's aunt was friendly, asked him to stay for lunch and brought a tray of treats to the room in the afternoon. Among other things, Gordon mentioned somebody he knew who had been able to get to Europe on a cattle boat. But how did you get from Burdock to the coast? They discussed the idea of riding the freights to Vancouver or Montreal. But what would there be to do in Europe, or even in Montreal? Neither one of the lads had even so much as ridden a streetcar.

When Bob went home in the late afternoon, he was more bewildered than ever.

Sometimes when the wheels of change have started to revolve in one's brain, big changes may be in the offing from different causes and other motivations. That is the way it seemed that night at the Benton supper table. Just when the three boys and Louisa had got settled into a nourishing bowl of chunky stew, mother Benton commenced to speak about a letter she had just received from the family lawyer. It concerned the final settlement and disposal of the remaining funds from the business and property at Quagmire. It had now been hanging fire for almost three years, but the trust company appointed by the courts was now ready to make a final liquidation.

"The chances for a crop of any kind this year or next look pretty bleak," she said. "I guess that is why they want to clean up the whole Quagmire mess at this time."

"Sure," interjected Norman. "No farmer has been able to pay off any old grocery bills lately. We can't expect that. But I bet the wholesalers all got paid off and the trust company will get its cut for liquidating everything."

"Well, boys, it doesn't matter what we think. We don't have the say. The estate lawyer thinks we are lucky. He says that there will be a final cheque for $4,850.00 deposited to our account down in the bank here, and that all that is needed now is my signature."

The sound of Four Thousand Dollars, while it was small compared to the moneys that had been dispensed, seemed almost like a bonanza from outer space after so many months of porridge and stewed meat. It didn't seem so much of a chore to accept, but it raised the question of how it could best be used to serve everybody.

At this point, Louisa had another surprise.

"You know, boys, I have been wondering just what is there left for us here in Burdock, anyway?"

She posed the question as though she was awaiting some answers. None came.

"Do you think the time has come when we should move?" she continued. "Why not sell this shack and buy a rooming house in Saskatoon?"

"Rooming house?" repeated Jamie. "Who wants to live in a big joint and smell all the stink from everybody's feet and their cooking? I'd sooner go back to Quagmire and live with the coyotes!!"

"But even the coyotes are starvin' at Quagmire," Norman snapped. "And since when did you get so fussy about smells, with all your muckin' around with weasel skins and gopher skulls? I say we should move."

Young Bob said nothing. His job at Feldman's was now full time as long as they were in business. If there were going to be changes on the Benton home front, he reasoned, perhaps he had better hang onto something more or less sure and keep one salary coming in until the rest got settled.

For the time being, the subject was dropped.

Monday morning Bob went back to his job at the old stand. There was a new shipment of work shirts and bib overalls to price-ticket, and some of the older stock had to be moved back into the shelves after the August clearance sale. Feldman was grumpy because the sale had been something of a flop. He had been making visits back and forth to the express office at the C.P.R. station and remarked that the flow of mail-orders from Eaton's and the Army and Navy mail order department was increasing while his volume was falling off. On Monday mornings, Feldman paced the floor a lot.

"Bob," he said, "when the store is closed this Wednesday after-noon, why don't you do something useful for the store? How would you like to take the grocery delivery truck down to Mike Jalnick's farm near Maxstone and pick up a half a pig he's butchering today? At least we'll get something on his overdue account."

"I have a better idea," answered Bob. "My friend Gordon Didgey goes out that way on trips with the telephone maintenance guy. I could go with them, pick up the meat and save the gasoline."

"Good thinking, lad! You work it your way, but remember, pork is food. Be sure to keep it wrapped and clean."

When the two boys climbed onto the telephone repair truck on Wednesday the air was calm, but a warm breeze was blowing in from the south. The previous day had been something of a howler, catching up billows of dry dust and sending it swirling into space. On the flat open plains there seemed little barrier, and when the powder-dry soil started to drift, only fence lines and the wind-breaks around farm buildings held the drifting silt. The boys hoped this would be a calmer day for a change.

Tommy Appleby was the telephone man. He was a sturdy young fellow who had been stringing wire and climbing poles since adolescence. In Gordon Didgey, the radio nut, he had found a kindred soul, so the trio made a compatible crew, and Appleby was glad to have the company. He was scheduled to go to Fife Lake on a call. Possibly they could pick up the pig carcass on the return trip.

But after relatively serene conditions, the wind increased. As they rattled along the highway, a meadowlark sat on a tumbleweed at the side of the road and commenced its bugled melody. But before it could finish the arpeggio, a gust of wind had hurled the tumbleweed into space and engulfed the lark in a cloud of flying silt. Three miles away, the elevators at Stonehenge were barely discernible—just misty skeletons against a dismal sky, clearing and becoming more dense with every whim of the wind.

The row of telephone poles at the side of the road appeared and disappeared as the truck passed over the next range of rolling hills and came out again on flat ground. To the left, a large field had stood fallow for more than its alloted time and was eroded almost to the subsoil. Recurring gusts of wind picked up silt and hurled it across the road to pile up in banks against the hedgerow of a farmer's yard. As they entered the towering cloud, they could hear the jingle of harness, the rumble of wheels and the clomp of horse-hooves on the road. A vehicle had come out of the driveway and crossed right in front of the truck before making a right-angled turn to go north. They hadn't seen nor heard a thing until they were parallel on the road.

"Whoah! Hold up there!" came a voice out of the gloom.

Tommy Appleby brought his slow-moving truck to a halt and pulled over to the right verge.

"How's the road to Burdock?" the voice asked. "Does this dust-bath last all the way, or just here on the flat?"

The vehicle was drawn by a team of scrawny horses. It was an uniquely designed contraption—a flat box bolted to the chassis of an old Ford touring vehicle. A glassed-in compartment covered the front seat while the rear portion was missing altogether. It was piled with gunny-sacks, filled and tied. The driver could direct the horses through an open slit in the window and watch the rubber-tired wheels bump along the road through a gaping hole in the old fender. It was just another version of the growing number of make-shift conveyances later known as "Bennett Buggies."

"Kind of a hell of a day to be going to town," Tommy shouted. "It's better, though, when you get over the ridge."

"That's all I wanted to know," the driver answered. "We bin sittin' here all weekend waitin' for a break an' we're gettin' short of groceries. It's pretty hard t' know when t' make the move."

"Well, how *did* you know this was the time?" Gordon queried with a smile.

"I tell yeh, young feller," the whiskery old face revealed. "We just toss a gopher up in the air on a morning like this. If he starts diggin', it ain't a fit day to go out. Are you fellers goin' t' the house? Our

telephone is on the blink y' know, an' the wife'll be glad t' see yez.''
And with that he pulled out onto the road.

Two minutes later, Tommy was out of his vehicle and approaching the front door of the weathered farmhouse. The heavy bedsheets that covered the south windows suddenly drew apart and three little faces appeared against the glass. When wind storms were at their worst, these sheets were kept wet in order to keep dust to a minimum in the house.

As the door swung open, they were greeted by a rumpled figure in a flowered housedress. Over her hair she wore a loose-fitting bonnet made from the matching remnants. "Am I ever glad to see you fellas!" she said. "We haven't been able to phone out since Friday."

Well, Tom Appleby fixed that phone and, as Gordon noted, it didn't take any great knowledge of electronics, either. The mechanism on the wall was so clogged with dust that the bell couldn't ring. Bob made conversation with the three tousled urchins and gladdened their day with three sticks of gum he found in his pocket. Meanwhile, their mother scurried around the room, damp cloth in hand, remarking incessantly that it was impossible to keep the place clean "while the banshee keeps blowin' his infernal breath through the walls. There niver was onnything like this in the Emerald Isle."

By the time the telephone repair truck had made its way through the enveloping dust clouds in the farm country and entered the ravines around Rockglen, they had treated two other phones with similar maladies, plus one with tightened sagging wires. The day was almost spent and they still had not made their call at Fife Lake. But why go to Fife Lake today? Another day the wind might have subsided and the going would be more pleasant. At Rockglen they decided to pull in at the Chinese cafe for a bite of lunch.

Down off the plateau, the village was partially sheltered from the sweep of the wind, but it showed signs of the district's erosion in cluttered gutters and buildings needing paint. Charlie Wong's Cafe was a familiar stopping place for Tommy Appleby, and he was greeted warmly by the proprietor at the front counter. There were the usual paintings on the wall, beautiful oriental landscapes and ornate pagodas, snow-white lilies in highly decorative vases and, in the window, a crossed-legged Buddha looking out over the empty street. Bob speculated that he might be contemplating the ancient beginnings of the Gobi Desert. The boys chose a booth in a corner next to the kitchen, one just next to a group of businessmen congregating for a chat.

It did not take long to make a choice, because the selection was somewhat limited. They wanted a lunch, not a meal. As the old saying went, the choice of pie was between "apple, laisin, mince—apple, laisin all gone," so they just ordered pie and ice cream with coffee. That came to a round twenty-five cents—enough 'til supper.

But while they were enjoying the rather tasty fare, fragments of conversation from the proxy Chamber of Commerce in the next booth came drifting over the low partition.

"George, you go down to the Kelly Drug Store in the afternoons, don't you?" one voice was asking. "That game of bridge that goes on in the back room must be going to your head if you're one of the people involved."

"Okay, Jack, come out with it. What are you getting at?"

Well, strange as it might seem, Jack (whoever he was), had got wind of a rumour that was floating around town. It seemed that a prospective customer had entered the Kelly Drug Store during the usual hour for the bridge game and had not been able to find a soul at the counter nor anyone to take her money. In the back room, of course, the game was in full session. Rumour also had it that the manager of the store was so engrossed in the game that he apparently forgot his role as salesmaker and boss.

"Hush," he is said to have counselled. "Just keep quiet for a few moments and maybe she'll go away."

"It's really come to a pretty pass," observed the ruffled Jack, "when the need to make every sale count and, if possible, add to the sale with suggestive ideas, has been overshadowed by the desire to make a grand slam at bridge. This will make a good subject for discussion at the next meeting of the Rockglen Board of Trade."

Bob privately wondered if this was one of the towns where the super-salesman from Swift's had sold his six cases of lunch tongue and so impressed Mr. Feldman.

They rose and left the cafe. Since the sun was setting, Tommy thought it was about time to start the trip back to Burdock. When they reached the plateau, the wind had subsided and they could now get a better look at the country they had driven through only a few hours and a few minutes before. Some landscapes looked like an arid waste-land that would never produce enough fodder to support even a gopher population. Where the soils were heavier, silt was piled against the fences and in many places only the top wires were visible. In every fence corner, and above the top level of the silt, were those long ribbons of tumbleweed caught on the wires and doing a ghost dance in the evening breeze.

The telephone repair truck pulled into the Jalnicki farm on its way through the Maxstone district and loaded a half carcass of pork, nicely wrapped and weighed. Feldman would be pleased in the morning. From what Bob and his friend Gordon Didgey had seen that afternoon, nature's healing processes would have to come soon or farmers could not even grow hogs to pay their grocery bills.

12

THE FINAL BLOW

*A*S a once-prosperous implement dealer in Burdock put it, anybody who had saved a nest-egg for a rainy day, saw it turn blue and smelly in the August heat. He may have been mixing his metaphors somewhat, but that was quite in character with the mixed-up thinking that came from wilted dreams and withered expectations. Nobody was in the mood anymore to buy anything but the essentials of life.

Nothing specific had been done about the Benton family's move to Saskatoon, although the need for a decision was pressing. The estate money was still sitting in the local bank, but one more winter of trying to exist near or at the poverty level might erode the last bit of capital they possessed. Up on the Saskatchewan River there would at least be some trees with leaves on them, heavier farmland that wouldn't go into orbit every time the wind blew, and there were students attending university who wanted to rent rooms. Louisa informed the boys that she was going to make some preliminary inquiries to the real estate advertisement she had been carrying in her purse for a week.

During the ensuing days, young Bob seemed to be walking around in a state of bewilderment. Did he really want to go? Down at Feldman's the employees had been reduced to a skeleton staff at the time of year when everything would usually be humming. One commercial traveller told Bob that it would be a good time for him to learn sign-painting and advertising layout in anticipation of the rash of bankrupt sales that would surely follow another crop failure. This kind of talk bugged him; and it bugged his friends, too. It smacked of an attempt to capitalize on calamity.

The only place they seemed to be able to escape this type of reverse rhetoric was at the dances in the curling rink building every Saturday night. The local band, which included his brother Norman on trumpet, had gone far beyond the greasy-kid stage and were trying to outripple Shep Fields, not to speak of Benny Goodman and Tommy Dorsey. There was also a rumour that Mart Kenny and his Silver Toned Seven would be coming to play at Woodriver Pavilion, and everybody was excited. Yes, the girls that turned up at these dances from Mossbank, LeFleche and Kincaid were enough to excite any young lad—at least they rated a flashy tie and a double splash of after-shave lotion.

It was nice to cut loose on Saturday nights. Most youngbloods on the prairie did. But when they returned to the work-a-day world on Monday, the problems were still there.

Gordon Didgey talked a lot about these things, and he was about the smartest young fellow Bob knew. In fact, he had once suggested that they should organize a discussion group and meet in his aunt's parlour every Sunday night after church. The idea was to get people with different points of view to come and join their "core group" for a wide-open discussion with no holds barred—the same way they had argued about evolution in high school. There would be plenty to talk about. The unemployed men from the work camps in B.C. were planning a march on Ottawa. Some said the Communists were behind it all. Why not get a Communist to come and explain what they hoped to accomplish? Then there were stories about the burning of oranges in California to prevent a glut on the market. Why couldn't they ship a carload or more to Burdock? And, it seemed the world had more wheat than could be sold, even though the grasshoppers kept it stripped to the ground from Central Butte to Texas. There were all kinds of subjects that could be discussed.

Well, it didn't take long for a subject of discussion to thrust itself before them for consideration. During the week, rumours began to spread about town that some local members of the Ku Klux Klan had rented the Alameda Hall, and a lawyer from Regina had been asked to come down and give an "enlightened lecture." Of course, the boys wouldn't be asking this lawyer to come to Mrs. Didgey's parlour, but they saw an opportunity to get to know who the local proponents were so that some time later they would know who to contact. There was a delicious Sherlock Holmes aspect about the whole affair that they somehow relished.

The night that Bob and Gordon went to the K.K.K. meeting, however, they left with a different feeling. It seemed as though they had been snooping into a closet where they could be sucked into further trouble and could put another dint into the battered peace of mind that they were trying to preserve. The hall was dimly lit. Most of the "officials" were out-of-towners, and the only people Bob could recognize was a cattle drover from the Quagmire district and a funda-mentalist minister from somewhere south of Limerick.

The lawyer started by saying that some of his best friends were Catholics and Jews, and that he didn't blame them individually for the tortuous road they were travelling. It was their *leaders* he wanted to nail against the wall for questioning. He claimed that the priesthood in Saskatchewan had been plotting since the days of Louis Riel, and were getting ready to take over whenever the Protestants got flabby and weakened their hold. With a sweep of his long arm, he declared that the "minions of the Pope have been putting down roots and breeding like jack rabbits."

"Many of the Protestants," he said, "are giving up their land in the Burdock district because of hard times—but not the Dogans. Some day they will swoop in on you from Gravelbourg, St. Victor and LaFleche and burn your churches to the ground. The only way they can be stopped," he concluded, "is through a clandestine group like the K.K.K. who will stand shoulder to shoulder, issue warnings, burn fiery crosses and stand ready to defend the Crown."

While the meeting was dealing with some thorny issues that had sprung from this diatribe, Gordon and Bob slipped out the door at the rear and walked in the direction of the Didgey home. There were multitudes of thoughts bubbling up in their minds. Neither said a word for about a block—possibly on the chance of being overheard.

"Well," Gordon muttered for openers, "do you think that crazy bunch of bastards can ever save us from the Black Plague?"

Bob didn't say much. His mind was too busy mulling over all of the inconsistencies. What would the Catholics do, he speculated, with all of the weatherbeaten houses and parched fields if they did move in? Does the Pope have some special magic for dealing with grasshoppers? What possible use is a bankrupt business to a starving half-breed rancher from Willow Bunch?

"You know," he ventured, "some of those gals from LaFleche who turn up at the curling rink dances on Saturday nights look like pretty choice woman-flesh to me. Maybe, if they breed like jack rabbits, us yokels here in Burdock have been missing out.''

That remark drew a snicker from Gordon, and by that time they were at the door of the Didgey residence.

"You know, Bob, your mother has just been over,'' Mrs. Didgey said as they entered the parlour. "Sit down and I'll fix you both something to eat.''

The food was delicious, as always. The conversation wandered from one thing to another, but there seemed to be something that the hostess was trying to introduce. Finally, when she saw the opening, she began, "Your mother has quite a dilemma, Bob. She was telling me that she is negotiating to buy a house in Saskatoon, and that the other boys are anxious to make the move, but that you are the one who is hanging fire. Are you really so in love with Burdock that you don't want to leave the place?''

"Did she tell you she'd bought the house?'' Bob asked in way of a feeler.

"Well, I think a deal is coming pretty well down to the wire if the letter she got today is any indication.''

That was all that Bob needed. It was time to level.

"You see, Mrs. Didgey,'' he began, "it's not just a matter of moving. The problem is whether you're going to land on your feet or on your head. Mother wants to go, and I don't blame her, but everything in Saskatoon will be a new ball game. She will have Norman and Jamie along to help. Norman has two ways to earn money. He's a sash and door maker and a darned good musician. Jamie still has one year to go in high school. There will be a shack left here in Burdock that has to be painted, shingled and sold. There is one Benton character who can keep working here, buy the paint and do the shingling. That guy is me.''

The usually placid Mrs. Didgey was somewhat taken aback with this version. "Well, this is something new to me,'' she ventured. "Is there anything the Didgey household can do to make your plans work out any better?''

But before there was time for a response, she cut in again with a burst of enthusiasm. "Now, there's no way you're going to live over there in that shack alone, existing on pork and beans and shingling the roof after hours. No! If your mother leaves in two weeks like she intimated, you're living with us here and that's decided. Gordon will be pleased to have a sidekick in the house, and he can help you paint. Just sit still there for a minute, and I'll give your mother a call.''

When she came back from the telephone, and before Bob had time to consider all of the options, the deal had been made and the contract sealed. Bob would pay eight dollars each week for board and room. If he wanted to slip Gordon a few dollars for helping at the painting and shingling once in awhile, that would be appreciated and help keep him in spending money. It was such a good arrangement that it seemed like old coulee days back at Quagmire when they had shingled the C.P.R. station together. And, oh, yes! There was another part of the contract. If they could find a buyer for the shack, they could split everything they got over two thousand dollars.

In the few days that followed, weather conditions did not improve. There had been only one shower that fall, and it came more as a teaser at the end of a sultry day. It sent expectations soaring temporarily, but after two more days of heat, the wind rose and clouds momentarily blocked out the sun.

It was during one of these dim-outs that a big truck arrived, loaded the contents of the Benton bivouac and made ready to take to the road. Louisa and Jamie rode in the cab with the driver. Norman crouched under a covered enclosure fashioned by himself among the beds and chairs. It was a good day to leave Burdock. With this kind of windy sendoff, they could depart with the least regret.

As the truck headed out past the grain elevators toward Moose Jaw and beyond, Bob followed it to the outskirts in the old delivery truck that he had borrowed from the store. By nightfall they would be unloading at the two-storey frame building Louisa had bought in Saskatoon. Bob just wanted to see them off. He turned in at the first side road and watched. The big transport lumbered northward through the usual cloud of dust and, caught up in the back eddy was a cortege of rolling tumbleweed.

That night in Burdock could have been an emotional downer to the last Benton left attached to the failing umbilicus of the southern plains. No doubt there were some pensive moments but, when the meal was over and they had taken some clothes to his room, the novelty of having a radio receiving set so close at hand was enough to transfer thoughts to other events. Here was a new contact with the outside world. One news item told how the march on Ottawa had gone sour, ending in violence at Regina. Then there was the amusing banter of Amos and Andy to listen to. What the hell! Tomorrow he would see how much discount Feldman would give him on three gallons of white paint.

When it came to buying the paint, the price was right, but there was still that problem of weather. How did you go about painting a house white in a dust storm? The answer was that you didn't. You gave up temporarily and tried shingling instead. Some of the old ones might blow away when torn off, but the big packs of new cedar shingles could be tied down on the roof with a rope while you nailed the individual shingles securely in place one by one. Gordon did a few rows in the early morning and they both worked in the evening after the wind had subsided.

The job went fast. After ten days of interrupted but persistent scheduling, the roof on the shack had been completely renovated. Next was to get all the brushes ready, the paint mixed and the scraping done in anticipation of a weather forecast promising two consecutive days of calm. Fortunately they came during Rosh Hashanah—the Jewish New Year—when Feldman's would be closed. In true Tom Sawyer style, Bob had recruited two of his mates to whom he had extolled the great soul-satisfying merits of house painting and, with four brushes dipping into the cans for the best part of one day, the job was accomplished with dispatch—gleaming white and completely free of flying particles of debris.

They were pleased. An accomplishment like that was worth a long-distance call to Saskatoon. Yes, they reported, the old bivouac looked like new. Yes, everything was going fine. No complaints. And in return they learned that the Saskatoon venture was working out well also—one room rented to a couple of bank clerks, two students setting up light housekeeping facilities and passing on the good word to fellow students. Everything seemed to be clicking.

Everything, that is, except the weather. Sure they had a respite, but if anybody thought that the prairie wind was about to shut down for the season, they were sadly mistaken. It was nearly the last week in September and the gusting had not ceased for more than four or five days in succession since the time the crops had wilted. Farmers were now praying for an early snow. No great depth of it, mind you—just a crust that would sit on top would be better than a light rain that would disappear like dew hitting a blotter.

It was just one week after the house-painting bee that Feldman called Bob into the office to suggest another of those special missions into the hinterland. Bob called them the Laura Secord expeditions, because they were usually to some dejected outpost to collect a bill, pick up some chickens on an account, deliver a few bolts of flowery muslin for a Rumanian wedding or possibly some linseed oil for an ailing horse. Bob usually got these jobs because, as Feldman said, he seemed to be dependable. This time it was to deliver a special black fedora to an Eastern Orthodox priest who had got the wrong size by mistake from the store and was holding back payment on his cheque until an exchange was made. At a cost of eight dollars and fifty cents, it was no trifling matter.

Bob would take the grocery delivery van again, gas it up on Wednesday morning and take the delivery boy along for company.

It was just going on eight that morning when the boys pulled out on the highway. The air was clear with a zephyr of breeze sending waves through the scattered strands of dry grass. The idle chit-chat that went on in the cab was not very stimulating, and the telephone poles clicked by with the monotonous precision of a metronome. Nearing Limerick, whoofs of powdery silt sifted across the highway in the path of their rattling Ford. At this point they took the side road heading south, now facing into the wind.

Down off the main thoroughfare, the rolling country south of Lakenheath had always held a strange fascination for Bob. Here the folds in the hills started to deepen into coulees snaking their way to Twelve-Mile Lake, and it was these ravines that sheltered the low-built farm buildings that seemed to hug the landscape. Many of the settlers here were from Eastern Europe and they had brought with them the traditional ways of the Carpathian valleys and lowlands. Loads of hay and cattle fodder were often stored on the flat roofs of sheds and barns. Chickens ran loose in the yards and the garden plots were a forest of poplar wands giving support to luscious hanging tomatoes, cucumber vines and clusters of yellow beans.

This is the picture Bob had in his mind from former visits. What assailed his eyes, however, was the dreary legacy of two years of unrelenting atmospheric assault—a devastation that was still in progress.

There were no hawks perched on the fence-posts, threatening mice in the grasses below. Only the occasional gopher sat up to note their passing. The low buildings seemed banked with silt. The super-hardy caragana hedges showed greenery, but they, too, were holding back banks of shifting topsoil. Farm yards were strewn with machinery, giving shelter to groups of chickens and small pigs, and occasionally an emaciated cow could be seen dragging her bony carcass to a green patch near the watering trough. In one place, both machinery and hayracks had been lined up along the creek to where the garden-plot had been moved. A pump lifted water out of the shrunken stream in an effort to fill out a crop of potatoes and root vegetables still in the ground. And this place seemed an oasis when compared with the cracked-open earth in the adjacent fields and the parched hills in the background.

It was not yet mid-morning and already the wind had got to the gusty stage. They were still travelling south and still passing those fence-lines piled high with Russian thistle, snapped off at the base of their stems and blown willy-nilly to get tangled in the first obstruction.

Pulling into the village of Flintoft, ten minutes later, they were hoping for a reprieve, but bits of paper, chaff, and clouds of dehydrated horse manure from the streets were swirling in circles around the buildings. Should they stop at the dejected-looking cafe where the sign was hanging askew from its moorings, or should they try to find the priest and get away as fast as possible? Maybe someone in the restaurant would know where he lived.

One touch to the door and it blew in, carrying a mess of dirt and airborne flotsom. The oriental countenance behind the counter smiled wanly. "You' truck say you from Burdock. Welcome to Flintoft. What you like fo' lunch, boy?"

There wasn't another soul in the building. Obviously he was trying for his first customer.

"We are looking to find Father Portescu," Bob announced. "But we could use some coffee or a glass of milk to wet our whistles."

While they were enjoying this small indulgence, the proprietor was busy with the broom. "Wind no good!" he ventured. "Ladge-hoppa no good, too. Farma clop all go now. Next winter Charlie all time sleep."

Charlie had summed it all up in one empty corn husk.

But the boys had no time to entertain gloom. In less time than the cafe owner would have preferred, they were saying goodbye and climbing a gentle slope to the parish residence. There was nobody in the street—only a stray dog digging into an overturned garbage can. Bob had once read about Transylvania and some of its spooky Dracula characters. The setting, at least, was appropriate.

When the door opened it did not creak. In fact, Father Portescu appeared as an amiable sort. He invited them in at once, recognized Bob from having talked with him one time at the store, and asked the delivery boy his name.

"Sandy Belcher," the lad replied. "I deliver the groceries, but not the hats. It must have been somebody else that goofed." He wanted to make that point clear.

The good father smiled and proceeded to pass the time of day at some length in his halting English before he brought the offending fedora to the room in a manila bag. Without hesitation, he drew it from its cover and placed the size 6¾ fur felt creation atop his oval Slavic head. The rim flipped up all way around and perched on his beaming countenance with bizarre indignity. It was a sight that could only draw laughter.

By the time Bob got around to unveiling what he had brought in the oval box, a tray of goodies had arrived from the kitchen. The boys nibbled, but the priest could not overcome his curiosity. As the new hat settled to the prescribed quarter-inch from the top of his left ear, he smiled with satisfaction. "Tell your boss he can cash the cheque," were his parting words.

They had been in the house for less than half an hour but, on emerging into the street, found that the scene had gotten even worse. The dog had abandoned his prize bits of garbage, and there were now sheets of newspaper and other debris blowing wildly against buildings and tangling around the telephone wires. The boys had previously been anxious to get back to Burdock in order to salvage as much of the Wednesday half-holiday as possible, but now they had an added sense of urgency. To the north, the sky was just a dull, grey backdrop. There was little time to waste loitering.

When you head out into a rainstorm, you know you can get stalled, wet or drenched. But heading into a maelstrom of prairie dust is like facing a howling blizzard of flying particles that are both raspy and unclean. The first mile was just a matter of finding the road and making sure that both verges were always in view; otherwise it would be like flying blind. Then, four to five miles farther, where they thought Lakenheath should be, there was not an elevator in sight— only a dark grey haze.

The engine on the old wheezer was hitting on all four cylinders— pumping a little oil, mind you, but chugging right along for a vehicle of such noble vintage. The density of the dust, however, appeared to be increasing, and all they could see now was two dim tracks and the occasional fence-post. Bob was about to stop temporarily and wait for a clearing of the view, when the headlights of an approaching vehicle appeared in the gloom, pulled over a few feet and continued on with a peep of its horn. At least he knew there was life out there.

Just to crawl along at a snail's pace seemed the safest course while the atmosphere was so murky and blinding. Up ahead, a giant cloud was rising into the heavens as though fed by some unseen turbulence of its own. The source was now apparent. To the left, a current of wind was coming up through a coulee draw that virtually acted like a wind-tunnel. The torrid blast caught up the dehydrated soil off a fallow field and hurled it aloft in great menacing shadows that drifted into the north-eastern skies.

Bob had to do something, so he headed the old van into this

dismal nightmare, dimming his headlights in order to regain sight of the gravelled road. Beside him sat a crouching Sandy with an old towel that he had pulled from the glove compartment. He must have thought he was an Arab tribesman tackling the Moroccan desert, because he was busy lapping the fouled old rag around his head in loose folds.

Dust was now coming up through the floorboards and billowing in through cracks in the panelled compartment behind the seat. Sandy discarded his towel as useless and was getting ready to light a cigarette. Bob couldn't believe it. He snatched the fag out of the kid's mouth and butted it out on the floor. It was now obvious that he had another problem. Feldman had done him no favour by sending this kid along— a grade nine drop-out with about as much spunk as a torpid toad. Now he sat sullen and just looking stunned.

Although the prospects looked grim, it was impossible to do anything but move ahead. If he could get to Limerick the main highway was wider and the possibilities of getting help, if needed, were better. Sometimes the filtering systems on these old cars would clog up with dust and leave you stranded. That was another thought that came to plague him. And, at that moment, another pent-up outburst came out of the left ditch and gave such a reef to the old car's hood that Bob thought it might lift right off. Each recurring squall went soaring off into the eastern sky like a demented banshee, scattering trash, weed-seeds and silt in careless abandon.

In the general melee, Bob noticed that there seemed to be a pattern to the whole blow, a series of squalls and then a momentary lull. He would try to adapt his rate of progress to these outbursts. A heavy foot on the accelerator took him through for a hundred yards or more, then a stall. When that blow let up, he tried for another gain. As the vehicle hurtled forward, a gust of wind hit his side door. This time it was carrying gravel and small stones. The steering wheel shimmied in his grip and he could feel a tug on the left front tire as it caught solid in the deeper aggregate and refused to respond to his direction. Within the cloud of dust that engulfed them, he could feel that they were now hopelessly off course. Down they went, hitting stones and minor obstructions until everything stopped in a dull thud. Something more effective than applied brakes had brought them to a full stop.

What a time and what a place to be marooned!!!

Bob stumbled out of his gaping door, missed his footing and tumbled awkwardly over a piece of shattered lumber. It was part of the guard-rail that had been used to protect the open mouth of a culvert. The damage seemed to be minimal, but the situation somewhat strange. Three wheels were still solidly on ground, but the left front fender was hanging in mid air and the wheel lazily turning in the breeze. The storm was enough to endure, but how were an off-duty shoe salesman and a muckle-headed kid supposed to extract them-selves from this mess?

At first they pondered the possibility of easing the vehicle back-ward by using blocks under the rear wheels and an old fencepost as a lever to lift the front end upward and back. This idea had to be abandoned when they could not find a post in the blinding storm. A scantling taken off the guard-rail was tried but was so dry that it snapped in two with the first heave. The atmosphere was so intolera-ble and Bob was getting so short tempered in the dirt and grime that he suggested they just get back in the cab for a while and do some thinking.

It must have been past the dinner hour by this time. A little food would have been eagerly accepted, but the need for something to drink seemed more pressing. Just to sit did not require much nourish-ment, but to be caged up in the heat and wind might test their sanity in time.

One hour passed and young Sandy began to fret. The questions were not exactly intelligent, but they came in a never-ending stream: What are we doing here, anyway? How will my dad know where we are? Did the steering gear break or didn't you know where you were going? Bob was nonplussed. He didn't know how far from Limerick they might be. The wind would most likely subside at sundown, but by that time this kid would have driven him mad. He was wracking his brain for some sort of an answer when, a half mile or so up ahead, he thought he could see the dim glow of headlights showing through the gloom. It was a vehicle approaching slowly from the north.

The two castaways watched it intently for a minute and Bob was preparing to clamber back up onto the road. But then everything went black behind another cloud of dust. When the air cleared again, there was a dim shaft of light moving now in a westerly direction. The driver must have turned off the main road and up a side alley—or possibly a laneway. The headlights made a wide circle and then came to a stop beside some dark structure. There must be farm buildings at that location.

"Well, what do we do now?" Bob asked. "Do you want to stay here or do you want to come with me?"

The answer came without delay. Both lads scrambled out of the cab as though they had been given a reprieve from the gallows. But even at this stage, Bob wasn't taking a chance. He had grabbed up a coil of rope that was lying on the floor in the back of the truck. "Tie that end to your belt,'' he said. ''I'll tie this end around my waist and that way I won't lose you.''

They were certainly more exposed on the open road than they had been in the cab. Vagrant whirlwinds swooped up particles of dirt that found access to collars, nostrils and eyes. Bits of clay and sharp sand pricked the bare shins like a thousand tiny needles. It seemed they had trudged almost half a mile, walking backwards part of the time and shielding faces with elbows. Bob was in the lead, following the verge of the old tire tracks, when he stumbled over a rash of gopher diggings and almost jerked Sandy off his feet at the other end of the tether. Here the gravel ended rather abruptly. Another road appeared to be entering from the west at a right-angle—or was this the expected laneway? Peering intently into the haze, they could see the outline of a gate and a dim light from a window back among the shadows.

Approaching the weather-beaten frame house, the two stragglers headed for the porch at the rear where a torn screen flapped about and the door stood partly ajar. An old black Chevy touring model stood in the yard, its lights now extinguished. There was a prompt answer to Bob's sharp knock. An old lady stood in the doorway, her greying hair piled high in a bun over two rather generous ears. She spoke through a set of loose-fitting dentures—not at the boys, but to the man in the background.

''Well, lands a caution, Densel, look what the wind blew in today!''

Densel soon appeared over her shoulder and took a squinting look at the lads over the top of the spectacles that teetered on his nose. It hadn't been long since he'd taken his cap off, because the shock of badger-coloured hair was still flattened against his forehead.

''Are youze fellers lost?'' he ventured. ''And, if you're sellin' anything, we got no money.''

Bob lost no time in explaining their predicament but, from the evidence he saw before him, knew there was little chance of getting the help he needed to get the impaled truck back off the culvert and onto the road. He spied a telephone on the wall and knew it had to be his best hope.

While Bob was busy negotiating the use of the phone with Densel, the old lady was eyeing Sandy up and down with more than passing interest.

''Are you one of the Belcher boys from Burdock?'' she asked with a smile. ''If you are, I know yer mother—been at yer house a good many times—looked after yer little sister when she had the croup.''

Sandy brightened up perceptibly. ''If this is Limerick,'' he said, "you must be Mrs. Doud. Mum says you're her best friend."

"Limerick's jist a mile up the road, dear," the old lady answered. "Just call me Auntie Muriel."

Well, that conversation was good for a pretty solid feed of pork hocks and sauerkraut with two glasses of buttermilk to wash it down. Bob was now a little repentant. This Sandy character wasn't a bad kid to know after all. In no time at all he got his phone call through to Feldman, and then there was nothing to do but to wait. He still felt drained from the whole episode, but Feldman's car would be along soon. They could just leave the old truck in the ditch until the weather cleared up, possibly in the morning.

Thursday morning at Feldman's department store was one to remember. The ill-fated expedition to Flintoft had possibly made Bob somewhat edgy, but in no way was he ready for this. The first two customers at the clothing counter were returning garments. And later he was called into the office to explain why he had let one of the garments out "On Approval" and then taken it back with soil marks all along the collar line of the shirt.

His next assignment was to take a pair of cheap pants down the street to a Mr. Harry Parfament who could be found living in rooms over the Chinese cafe, better known as the Crown Royal. Under no circumstances was he to leave the parcel without having tucked the $3.95 into the pocket of his own pants.

There was a whole crowd of new people now living in the rooms up over the Crown Royal—possibly twenty to thirty of them, counting women and kids. They had been there for over a month now, waiting to see who was going to pay their passage back to England—the Government of Saskatchewan, the people at Ottawa, or the C.P.R.?

Several years earlier, they had been brought out as immigrants. It had been explained to them that a rich farming area was about to be opened for development in the district bordering on Montana and that "good British stock" was preferred. The railroad company would be building a spur line to haul out all of the grain crops and produce. Immigrants, even factory workers from the Lancashire Mills area who had never lived on a farm, it was alleged, would be able to buy land with the generous wages earned in rail construction. With determination and hard work, a new and prosperous life could be carved out on the Saskatchewan frontier.

Well, after four years of drought and deprivation, they had had enough. They were a rough and ready crew when it came to struggling, but they were not going to sit on the barren hills in a few shacks and eat gophers to stay alive. To force the issue and make officialdom face up to what they thought was its responsibility, this group of militants had moved to Burdock, found lodgings in the cheapest accommodation available and asked the proprietors to bill the government. The landlords had little to lose because the rooms were seldom occupied at any rate. It was a gamble they were willing to take.

When Bob arrived at the Crown Royal with his parcel, the wooden staircase up to the rooms on the second floor was strewn with litter. Three men sat in the doorway at the street level and rolled cigarettes, while a harum-scarum bunch of kids kept running in and out playing hopscotch on the sidewalk.

He edged his way through this gamut of disorder and had started to mount the squeaky stairs when he saw a tousle-headed woman leaning against the banister in conversation with some voices in the adjoining rooms. Just recently out of bed, her auburn hair looked like a rat's nest, and she had not yet bothered to get past the nightgown stage of undress. Two long and pendulous breasts hung low behind the dingy gown which barely hid her bare feet.

"The old perisher can't take it like 'eh used ter," she was boasting. "Ee's 'ad a chance t' make a quid or so deliverin' sale sheets fer the grocer down street, but the way ee's snorin' right now, ee'll be under bluddy sheets 'til after tea."

"Maybe the poor lad's sick," suggested a toothless biddy one door down the hall. "There's note to keep a man's spirits up around 'ere."

Another voice chimed in, "'ee didn't look too good yistiday, Mrs. Parfament. Maybe 'ee *is* sick."

Mrs. Parfament stood her ground. She braced her bare feet on the floor, turned both palms outward on her ample hips and snapped, "'ee's not sick, I've told ye, 'ee's indisposed—I've shagged 'im blind."

With that remark ringing in his ears, young Bob retreated down the stairs. In that condition, he surmised, Mr. Parfament wouldn't be needing the pants anyway. At least, he wouldn't be able to pay for them today.

While retracing his route to the store, Bob wondered how he was going to explain the unexpected loss of a clothing sale to the head of the Feldman merchantile establishment. Feldman always wanted to know the reasons.

Bob entered through the back door and proceeded to his clothing counter. But as he passed his esteemed and pampered shoe department, another strange scene assailed his eyes. Three of Mrs. Parfament's sister militants were comfortably ensconsed on the newly upholstered shoe benches, leisurely breast-feeding their babies. It was a much quieter environment for nursing little nippers than the Crown Royal Cafe.

That was the last straw. All of the display techniques that he had gleaned from the *Shoe and Leather Journal of Canada*, and the articles on "how to keep your selling space bright and inviting" had either been too successful or he had gone nuts. Bob gave it twenty minutes of serious thought and went to the office to tender his resignation. Maybe the life of a salesman was not in his cards.

Seven days later, and on another dusty Thursday, Robert Benton was catching a bus for Saskatoon. During the week, his friend Gordon Didgey had revealed that a job had opened up for him in the electronics department of a new radio station that would be coming on the air from Calgary. Carl Ericson had phoned from Wood Mountain to say that his uncle in Kingston, Ontario, was going to stake him to a term at Queen's University. The crowd at the Crown Royal were not the only people on the move. There seemed to be a general exodus in progress.

As the big grey bus rolled up the highway toward Moose Jaw, it was escorted by a pall of dust and litter. Following closely in the back-eddy came the usual cortege of tumbleweed, doing acrobatic somersaults and scattering seeds over any soil that offered succor.

Weeds, we are reminded, are defined as varieties of vigorous and persistent plants growing in the wrong place at the wrong time.

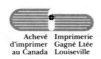

Achevé   Imprimerie
d'imprimer Gagné Ltée
au Canada Louiseville